THOMAS HARDY
Behind the Inscrutable Smile

ANDREW NORMAN

HALSGROVE

First published in Great Britain in 2004

Copyright © 2004 Andrew Norman

Front cover picture: *Thomas Hardy in 1906.*
Photo: Dorset County Museum.

Frontispiece picture: *Thomas Hardy, from an
original oil painting by Jean Norman.*

British Library Cataloguing-in-Publication Data
A CIP record for this title is available from the British Library

ISBN 1 84114 324 3

HALSGROVE

Halsgrove House
Lower Moor Way
Tiverton, Devon EX16 6SS
Tel: 01884 243242
Fax: 01884 243325
email: sales@halsgrove.com
website: www.halsgrove.com

Printed and bound by
The Cromwell Press, Trowbridge

Contents

About the author

Andrew Norman was born in Newbury, Berkshire, England in 1943. In 1956 his family moved to Southern Rhodesia (now Zimbabwe) and so witnessed the closing years of the colonial era. In 1959 the family returned to England, and in 1962 he went up to Oxford University, to St Edmund Hall. Having graduated in physiology he became a medical student at The Radcliffe Infirmary; qualifying as a doctor in 1970. He married in 1967 and has a son and daughter. In 1972 he went into general practice in Poole, Dorset. A serious back injury in 1983 forced his early retirement, and he is now a writer.

His other books include:-

HMS Hood: *Pride of he Royal Navy* – Stackpole Books, Mechanicsburg, P.A. U.S.A. (2001) – ISBN 0-8117-0789-X.

By Swords Divided: Corfe Castle in the Civil War – Halsgrove, Tiverton, U.K. (2003) – ISBN 1-84114-228-X.

Robert Mugabe and the Betrayal of Zimbabwe – McFarland & Company, Inc. Publishers, Jefferson, North Carolina, U.S.A. (2004)
– ISBN 0-7864-1686-6.

T.E. Lawrence: Unravelling the Enigma – Halsgrove, Tiverton, U.K. (2003)
– ISBN 1-84114-321-9.

Tyneham: the Lost Village of Dorset – Halsgrove, Tiverton, U.K. (2003) –
ISBN 1-84114-322-7.

Preface

Did Thomas Hardy ever smile? Certainly he did, and to prove it there exists a photograph of him (taken in an unguarded moment), with a twinkle in his eye and a broad smile on his face! However, as a very private person who detested reporters and photographers, it is hardly surprising that almost every other image shows him with a serious face.

Hardy was shy to a fault. He surrounded his house with a dense blanket of trees; he took immense pains to disguise the characters of his novels and the places they frequented even though, as he said himself, everything he wrote had a basis in fact. (He did this not deliberately to mislead people, but out of an almost paranoid fear that through them, the public would discover the real Thomas Hardy.) In his later years he destroyed the 'evidence' – as it were – letters, notebooks, and diaries, not only his, but also those of his first wife, Emma. Even his second wife Florence's so-called 'biography' of him was virtually entirely dictated by him to her. And yet, unbeknown to the outside world, the drama which Hardy was experiencing in his own life was equal in tension and excitement to anything we might find in his novels!

Imagine a young man aged twenty-nine, a trainee architect, being sent in the year 1870 to North Cornwall to plan and oversee the restoration of a church which had fallen into disrepair. He travels down from Dorset to that wild and romantic place; knocks on the door of the church's rectory, and is greeted not by the rector, but by the rector's wife's sister, a strikingly attractive young woman of the same age as himself, with blue eyes and flowing locks of red hair. For Thomas Hardy – for this is the young man in question – it is love at first sight.

The couple's courtship lasts for a period of over four years, during which time they are able to meet only rarely, on account of the distance. As a result of this acquaintance – brief in terms of time actually spent together – Hardy marries a woman whose character he knows virtually nothing about. By the time their honeymoon is over, a deep and unbridgeable gulf has opened up between them. The trauma of this ill-considered match is long-lasting; and the effect on Hardy's psyche, well-being, and outlook is catastrophic. Even Emma's death cannot assuage his grief, nor give him relief from his inner pain. So where did it all go wrong?

Hardy's relationship with Emma is one of the most fascinating aspects of his life. Not only would it profoundly influence his outlook and philosophy; we also see it reflected in the plots of his novels, and in the sentiments expressed in his poems.

My interest in Thomas Hardy was awakened when I discovered that my ancestors on my father's side once lived at Fordington on the outskirts of Dorchester, Dorset (Fordington being only 2 miles from Higher Bockhampton, Hardy's family home). They were baptised, married, and buried at its parish church of St George, by the vicar the Reverend Henry Moule. Moule's son, Horatio Mosley Moule (known as Horace), became Hardy's mentor and his dearest friend; indeed perhaps the most formative influence on his life and career.

The purpose of this book is to pierce the veil of secrecy which Hardy deliberately drew over his private life, and thereby to discover the true Hardy, the man behind the inscrutable smile! My journey of discovery led me to explore his old haunts, in particular his house (he disliked it being called a cottage) at Higher Bockhampton, and artefacts connected with him – including the contents of his study – which are to be found at the Dorchester County Museum, also St Juliot, where he met and courted Emma.

Acknowledgements

I am grateful to the Director, Dorset County Museum, Dorchester, for permission to use in the text, photographs of Thomas Hardy and his family and friends, and also to reproduce contemporary watercolours by Henry Moule. Also to volunteers Gwen Yarker, Lilian Swindall and Judith Stinton.

I would also like to thank Mrs Jean Norman for allowing me to reproduce her oil painting of Thomas Hardy as the frontispiece. Also Jane Norman, Thomas Norman, Tom Gillibrand, Peter Devlin, and Michael, Nicholas and Nina Dragffy.

Also the librarians of the British Library; University of Bristol; Magdalene College, Cambridge; and the librarians and staff of Poole, Swanage, Wareham, Canford Cliffs, and Dorchester libraries.

My thanks are also due to the Clarendon Press, Oxford; Cassell and Company Ltd, London; Mid Northumberland Arts Group and Carcanet New Press; Oxford University Press; Macmillan Publishers Ltd; The Hogarth Press, London; David & Charles Ltd, London; MacGibbon & Kee, London; The Toucan Press, Guernsey; Longman Group Ltd; Colby College Press, Maine, U.S.A.; Professor Michael Millgate, Toronto, Ontario, Canada.

I am especially grateful to Rachel Dragffy for her invaluable help and encouragment.

1

Parents and Forebears: Environment: Immediate Neighbours

Hardy's maternal grandmother Elizabeth Swetman of Melbury Osmond, a hamlet in north-west Dorset situated on the boundary of Lord Ilchester's estate, was descended from a family of landed yeomen (small, freeholder farmers). She possessed a library of thirty or so books (which was highly unusual for one of a relatively low station in life), and was familiar with the writings of Joseph Addison (essayist), Sir Richard Steele (essayist and dramatist) and others of the *Spectator* (magazine, founded 1828) group: also with John Milton (poet), Samuel Richardson (novelist) and John Bunyan (preacher and author). Elizabeth had an excellent memory and could be relied upon by the parson to identify in cases of doubt, any particular grave in the church-yard. She was of a romantic disposition, and was skilled in ministering to the sick of the locality – her authority being the English herbalist Nicolas Culpepper's (1616-54) *Herbal and Dispensary*. Her ten volumes of Henry Fielding's (novelist and dramatist) Works would one day pass to her famous grandson, Thomas Hardy. [1.1]

Elizabeth met and secretly married a servant, one George Hand, of whom her father John disapproved to the extent that she was disinherited by him. When, soon after her father's death, Elizabeth's husband also died, she and her seven children were left destitute. One of these children, Jemima, born at No. 1, Barton Close, Melbury Osmond in 1813, was destined to become the mother of the famous author who is the subject of this book.

๑๑

Hardy's paternal great-grandfather John Hardy (born 1755), came from the village of Puddletown, 2 miles north-east of Higher Bockhampton, and 5 miles north-east of Dorchester, Dorset's county town. A mason, and later a master mason and employer of labour, John married Jane Knight and the couple had two sons, Thomas (born 1778) and John.

This Thomas Hardy (I), 'somewhat improvidently married' at the age of twenty-one, a Mary Head from Berkshire; a person who had known great hardship as a child through being orphaned. [1.2] Thomas' father, John, duly came to the rescue by building for his son, in 1800-1, the house at Higher Bockhampton, on land leased by the Kingston Maurward estate. (In those days a man with sufficient means could erect a dwelling for himself, or for a relative, and be thereafter permitted to live there for their lifetime: such a person being called a 'livier'.) Also included were two gardens (one part orchard), a horse paddock, sand and gravel pits, and 'like buildings'. [1.3]

Thomas Hardy I carried on the family tradition by following the same occupation as his father. Like all the members of his family, it was his firm belief that the Hardys were descended originally from the 'Le Hardy' family of Jersey in the Channel Islands, John le Hardy having settled in Weymouth in the fifteenth century. He also believed that they were distantly related to Admiral Sir Thomas Masterman Hardy (who served under Horatio Nelson as flag-captain of HMS *Victory* in the Battle of Trafalgar). There appeared, however, to be no documentary evidence to back up these claims. [1.4] Thomas I and his wife Mary had six children, the oldest being Thomas Hardy (II, born 1811).

Under Thomas II the family business flourished, with as many as fifteen men being employed by him, including the 'tranter' who carried the materials to the building sites.

∽

Elizabeth Hand's daughter Jemima had worked as servant and cook in several Dorset houses, and also in London; she was also skilled at tambouring (embroidering) gloves, and mantua (gown) making. Since late in 1836, Jemima had been cook to the Reverend Edward Murray, vicar of Stinsford's church of St Michael (Stinsford being a hamlet situated less than a mile from Higher Bockhampton). Murray was in the habit of inviting violin players Thomas I and his son Thomas II to musical evenings at his residence, Stinsford House, adjoining the church, and this is possibly where Thomas II met Jemima. The couple were married on December 22, 1839 at her mother's family's church at Melbury Osmond.

Thomas Hardy II.
Photo: Dorset County Museum.

Jemima Hardy.
Photo: Dorset County Museum.

When she married Thomas II, Jemima was already more than three months pregnant. In those days, however, conception before marriage was considered by the Dorset farm labourers (and even by the lower middle classes) to be nothing unusual. In fact, the marriage did not normally proceed until the pregnancy had become obvious! There was a good reason for this. It was essential that a woman prove her ability to have children, who from an early age would be required to help support the family. In those days, it was not unusual to see eight-year-olds working in the fields. [1.5] It would be presumptuous of any man or woman to believe that they could describe Thomas Hardy's house and its surroundings better than the great man himself, for later, at the tender age of sixteen, he obliged in this task by composing the poem 'Domicilium', which reads as follows:-

Domicilium
It faces west and round the back and sides
High beeches, bending, hang of veil of boughs,
And sweep against the roof. Wild honey sucks

10

Climb on the walls, and seem to spout a wish
(If we may fancy wish of trees and plants)
To overtop the trees hard by.

Red roses, lilacs, variegated box
are there in plenty, and such hardy flowers
As flourish best untrained. Adjoining these
Are herbs and esculents, and farther still
A field; then cottages with trees, and last
The distant hills and sky.
Behind, the scene is wilder. Heath and furze
Are everything that seems to grow and thrive
Upon the uneven ground. A stunted thorn
Stands here and there, indeed; and from a pit
An oak uprises, springing from a seed
Dropped by some bird a hundred years ago.

In days bygone –
Long gone – my father's mother, who is now
Blest with the blest, would take me out to walk.
At such time I once inquired of her
How looked the spot when first she settled here.
The answer I remember, 'fifty years
Have passed since then, my child, and change has marked
The face of all things. Yonder garden plots
And orchards were uncultivated slopes
O'ergrown with bramble bushes, furze and thorn:
That road a narrow path shut in by ferns,
Which, almost trees, obscured the passer-by'.

'Our house stood quite alone,
and those tall firs
And beeches were not planted. Snakes and ells (?eels)
Swarmed in the summer days, and nightly bats
Would fly about our bedroom. Heathcroppers
Lived on the hills,
and were our only friends;
So wild it was when first we settled here.'

Hardy's birthplace, by Henry Moule. Photo: Dorset County Museum.

View of Rainbarrow, by Henry Moule. Photo: Dorset County Museum.

Turning to more practical matters, the house where Hardy was born in 1840 was situated at the end of a leafy lane, bordered by thatched cottages. To be found on the grass verges of this lane on warm summer evenings were glow-worms, which Hardy would one day mention in his novel *The Return of the Native* – men used the glow-worms to enable them to see in the dark whilst playing dice on Rainbarrow (a tumulus – or ancient burial mound) on the heath.

Entrance to the house was through a porch leading directly into the kitchen, which had a deeply recessed fireplace on its south wall. Adjacent to it was the parlour, and then a small office where three generations of Hardys, who were stonemasons-cum-builders, did their accounts and kept their money. Their workmen were handed their wages through a tiny, barred window, little more than a foot square, situated at the rear. From the office an open staircase led up to the first floor, which had two bedrooms. These upstairs rooms, being built into the eaves, had sloping ceilings.

The house had a chimney at each end and was thatched with wheat straw. The walls were made of cob (a composition of clay and straw), with a brick-facing at the front. The ground floor was paved with Portland stone flagstones; the first floor with floorboards of chestnut 7" wide. Candles were used for lighting as was usual in those days.

At some later date, a self-contained bedroom and kitchen were added, the materials used being of inferior quality to those used in the construction of the original dwelling. This may have been after 1837, in order to provide accommodation for Thomas I's wife, Mary, when she was left a widow. Certainly, Mary appears in the 1851 census as living in the parish of Stinsford (of which Higher Bockhampton was part), rather than in Puddletown. Later still, perhaps after Mary's own death in 1857, the two buildings were conjoined.

෴

Thomas III was born in the main bedroom (the one above the office) of the Bockhampton house on 2 June, 1840, his entry into the world being an occasion of some drama. In fact it was only the quick wittedness of the 'monthly nurse' (who attended women during their confinement), that saved his life. Otherwise the world might have been deprived of one of its greatest writers, for at his birth, the infant Thomas was 'thrown aside as dead'! 'Dead! Stop a minute,' cried the nurse as she came to the rescue, 'he's alive enough, sure!' As for his infancy, the only event of note appears to be when his mother one day discovered him asleep in his cradle inside the house, with 'a large snake curled upon his breast' – which was also asleep! [1.6]

Jemima Hardy and infant Thomas.
Photo: Dorset County Museum.

꩜

The following year Thomas III's sister Mary was born, but it would be another decade before Henry (born 1851) arrived on the scene, to be followed in 1856 by Katharine. The two sisters would one day enrol for teacher-training at Salisbury, before taking up teaching posts at local schools. Henry, however, would carry on the family building business.

꩜

In 1844, when Thomas III was aged four, a monument was erected to his (presumed) ancestor Admiral Thomas Masterman Hardy, on Blackdown Hill, 7 miles away to the west, and this could be seen by Thomas III from his bedroom window.

꩜

Behind the house extended a huge area of heathland which was dotted with isolated cottages. This was subsequently given the name Egdon Heath by Hardy. On its south side lay Thorncombe Wood, which was bisected by the Roman road linking Dorchester (Durnovaria, two miles distant) with London (Londinium) via Badbury Rings and Salisbury (Old Sarum). Hardy would one day write a poem about this road: 'The Roman Road runs straight and bare/ As the pale parting-line in hair...'

Here are to be found swallet holes (hollows in the ground formed by the slow erosion of underlying layers of chalk by acidic water passing through from the surface gravels). Crossing Thorncombe Wood was an iron fence marking the Victorian estate boundary; also Rushy Pond, one day to be the subject of another poem by Hardy.

Beyond the wood lies the River Frome meandering through a fertile valley, with the distant ridge of the Purbeck Hills in the background. Ten miles to the south lies the town of Weymouth. On the periphery of the wood on the south side was the hazel coppice; this crop being specifically grown for the hurdle-making industry. The coppice provided inspiration for yet another poem–one of his most famous – 'The Darkling Thrush'.

In the seven other houses in the adjacent lane, known as Cherry Alley, there lived people of some standing in the community. These included 'two retired military officers, one old navy lieutenant, a small farmer (presumably it was his farm which was small, rather than he himself!) and tranter, a relieving officer (superintendent of relief for the poor) and registrar, and an old militiaman, whose wife was the monthly nurse that assisted him – Thomas Hardy – into the world'. [1.7] On such people as these, some of the characters in Hardy's novels would one day be modelled.

2

Pre-School Days: Music: First School

Even in those early years it was becoming increasingly clear that the young Thomas Hardy was a boy with an acutely sensitive nature. Nevertheless, although he was considered a delicate child, and therefore not sent to school until he was eight (instead of five, which was the normal practice), according to his sister Katharine, he was able to read by the age of three. On Sundays, when the weather was considered too wet for him to attend church, he would don a tablecloth, read Morning Prayer while standing on a chair, and recite 'a patchwork of sentences (normally) used by the vicar'.

Another of his favourite occupations was to lie on his back in the sun, cover his face with his straw hat, and think 'how useless he was'. He decided, based on his 'experiences of the world so far...', that 'he did not wish to grow up... to be a man, or to possess things, but to remain as he was, in the same spot, and to know no more people than he already knew', which was about half a dozen! [2.1] At other times he would 'go alone into the woods or on (to) the heath... with a telescope...', and 'stay peering into the distance by the half-hour...' or in hot weather, lie 'on a bank of thyme or camomile with the grasshoppers leaping over him.' [2.2] When, one cold winter's day, he discovered the body of a fieldfare in the garden, and picked it up and found it to be 'as light as a feather', and 'all skin and bone...', the memory remained to haunt him. The death of this small bird revealed not only Hardy's love of animals, but also his sense of the frailty of life itself. [2.3]

Jemima Hardy was very much a person who had her feet on the ground, so to speak. As Thomas III recalled in later years, it was 'Mother's notion (and also mine) that a figure stands in our van (path) with arm uplifted, to knock us back from any pleasant prospect we indulge in...'. [2.4] Jemima had inherited from her mother a love of books, and a desire to read every one she could lay her hands on, and under her influence it seemed inevitable that her own offspring, the young Thomas Hardy III, would follow in their footsteps. This was reinforced by such people as Mr King, the boy's godfather, who presented him at the tender age of seven with a volume entitled, *The Rites and Worship of the Jews*, by Elise Giles. [2.5]

☙

The conclusion of those around him was that young 'Tommy' would be 'no good for any practical pursuit', so therefore he would 'have to be a parson' – remarks which caused his mother Jemima 'many misgivings'. [2.6]

☙

Thomas Hardy I, in his early years at Puddletown, played the bass viol (viol being a forerunner of the violin) in the string choir of the village's church of St Mary, and he also assisted other choirs, at a time when music was traditionally produced by musicians occupying the raised 'minstrels' gallery', at the end of the nave. Having married Mary Head he moved into the house at Bockhampton, provided for him by his father, and from that time attended the local thirteenth-century church of St Michael, a mile away at Stinsford. Here, he began as a chorister and ended up playing the tenor viol. He was also much in demand to perform at 'weddings, christenings, and other feasts'. [2.7]

Thomas Hardy I discovered, on attending Stinsford church, that music there was provided not, as was the case at Puddletown, by a group of 'minstrels', but by 'a solitary old man with an oboe'. [2.8] He therefore, with the help of the elderly local vicar, the Reverend Floyer, set about remedying the situation. He gathered together some other like-minded instrumentalists, and from the year 1801, when he was aged twenty-three, until his death in 1837, conducted the church choir and played his bass viol at two services every Sunday.

After his death in 1822, the Reverend Floyer was succeeded by the Reverend Edward Murray, who was himself an 'ardent musician' and violin player. Thomas Hardy I, and his sons Thomas II and James, together with their brother-in-law, James Dart, practised with him two or three times a week at Stinsford House – where he chose to live, instead of at the rectory. Fourteen years later, Jemima Head would become the Reverend Murray's cook, and this is how she met her husband-to-be, Thomas Hardy II – as already stated. Practice sessions were also held at the house at Bockhampton, in addition to which there

17

were further duties to be performed at Christmas-time, including the onerous task of making copies of carols to be played.

On Christmas Eve it was the custom for the choir, composed of 'mainly poor men and hungry', to play at various houses in the parish, then return to the house for supper, only to set out again at midnight to play at yet more houses. [2.9] (These characters and occasions would one day be brought back to life by Thomas III, in *Under the Greenwood Tree*, and *The Mellstock Choir*.)

Thomas Hardy I's son, Thomas II, is described as being devoted to church music, but also to the 'mundane' – that is, 'country dance, hornpipe, and ... waltz'. As for his wife, Jemima, she loved to sing the songs of the times, including, 'Isle of Beauty', 'Gaily the Troubadour', and so forth. [2.10] However, although the family possessed a piano, and the children practised on it, she herself was unable to play.

A diagram (drawn by Thomas III with the help of his father), shows the relative positions of the members of the Stinsford church choir (singers and musicians) in about 1835. At the rear of the west gallery were singers ('counter' – high alto), and James Dart (counter violin). In the middle row were singers (tenor), Thomas Hardy II (tenor violin), James Hardy (treble violin) and singers (treble). In the front row were singers (bass), Thomas Hardy I (bass cello) and singers (treble), and finally there were more singers situated behind them all, in the church tower. [2.11]

But what of the young Thomas Hardy III. He would never have the pleasure of meeting his grandfather and namesake, who died in 1837, three years before he himself was born. Nevertheless, he inherited the family gift for making music, and was said to be able to tune a violin from the time that he was 'barely breeched' (put into trousers, which replaced the dress which was common attire for both infant boys and girls alike). [2.12]

When he was aged four, his father gave him a toy concertina, inscribed with his name and the date. Said to have an 'ecstatic temperament', his sensitivity to music manifested itself at this time in an extraordinary way. Of the numerous dance tunes played by his father of an evening, and 'to which the boy danced a 'pas seul' (dance for one person) in the middle of the room', there were always 'three or four that always moved the child to tears'. They were: 'Enrico', 'The Fairy Dance', 'Miss Macleod of Ayr' and 'My Fancy Lad'. Hardy would later confess that 'he danced on at these times to conceal his weeping'. [2.13]

As Thomas III grew older, he learned, under the instruction of his father, to play the violin and soon, like his forefathers before him, was much in demand on this account. Hardy always referred to the instrument as a 'fiddle', and to those who played it as 'fiddlers'. [2.14] Although his mother insisted that he must not accept payment for his services, he did on one occasion succumb to temptation and, with the 'hatful of pennies' collected, he purchased a volume entitled, *The Boys' Own Book*, of which his mother Jemima disapproved, since it was mainly about games. [2.15]

☙

In 1848, Thomas III arrived early at school for his first day of lessons and awaited 'tremulous and alone' the arrival of the schoolmaster, the schoolmistress and his fellow pupils. [2.16] Years later, he was to remember this first day in a poem entitled 'He Revisits His First School'.

The Bockhampton National School, which had been newly opened in that same year, was situated a mile or so across the fields from his house, beside the lane which led from Higher to Lower Bockhampton. It was the brainchild of Julia Augusta Martin who, with her husband Francis, the squire, had purchased the adjoining estate of Kingston Maurward from the Pitt family three years earlier, in 1845. The couple inhabited the manor house, built in the early Georgian period, and not to be confused with the estate's other manor house nearby, which dated from mid-Tudor times. Benefactress of Stinsford and Bockhampton, Julia Martin had built and endowed the school at her own expense, collaborating with the Reverend Shirley on the project.

The Martins had no children of their own, and Julia had singled out Thomas III for her affections, long before he had even started school. 'Passionately fond of Tommy', though she was thirty years his senior, Julia was 'accustomed to take (him) into her lap, and kiss (him) until he was quite a big child'! He, in turn, 'made drawings of animals in watercolours for her', and sang to her; one of his songs being, 'I've journeyed over many lands, I've sailed on every sea'. [2.17] That Thomas III recipro-

19

The old, Tudor, Kingston Manor House, by Henry Moule.
Photo: Dorset County Museum.

cated Julia Martin's sentiments is borne out by his statement, made some years later, that the lady in question was 'his earliest passion as a child'. [2.18]

It is said that at school, he excelled at arithmetic and geography, 'though his handwriting was indifferent'! [2.19] Meanwhile, his mother encouraged him with the gift of John Dryden's translation of Virgil, Dr Samuel Johnson's *Rasselas*, and a translation of St Pierre's *Paul and Virginia*; and a friend gave him the *New Guide to the English Tongue*, by Thomas Dilworth. [2.20] The young Thomas III also possessed *A Concise History of Birds*. Perhaps, however, his greatest joy was to discover in a closet in the house, a magazine entitled 'A History of the (Napoleonic) Wars'. [2.21] This would one day inspire Thomas III to write two books of his own, namely, *The Trumpet Major*, and *The Dynasts*.

When, a year later, Thomas III's parents decided that their son should transfer to a day-school in Dorchester, Mrs Martin was offended, not only at the loss of her 'especial protegé' 'little Tommy', but also because this new school was nonconformist (i.e. not Church of England). This may have been a deliberate gesture of defiance by the Hardys, who had a great antipathy towards the vicar, the Reverend Shirley, for destroying not only the fabric of their cherished Stinsford church, but also its cherished traditions including its live music.

&c

It was at about this time that Thomas III had his first experience of rail travel, the railway having come to Dorchester only as recently as 1847. This was when he and his mother Jemima (who often made excursions together) went to visit her sister in Hertfordshire, and on the return journey, caught the train from Waterloo Station, London, to Dorchester.

3
Dorchester: Church: Young Love: The Darker Side of Life

At the age of nine, Thomas Hardy III commenced the second stage of his formal education. He attended a day school in Dorchester, walking there and back each day, a distance of 6 miles in all. Here he flourished, winning at the age of fourteen his first prize, a book entitled *Scenes and Adventures at Home and Abroad*. [3.1]

The headmaster, Isaac Last, was by repute 'a good scholar and teacher of Latin', but because this subject was not part of the normal curriculum, Thomas III's father was obliged to pay extra for it. Nevertheless, his confidence in his son was amply rewarded when, in the following year, the boy was awarded Theodore Beza's *Latin Testament* for his 'progress in that tongue'.

Other authors with whom Thomas III was familiar were William Shakespeare, John Bunyan, Walter Scott, Alexander Dumas, Harrison Ainsworth, James Grant and G.P.R. James. [3.2] He also commenced French lessons, and at the age of fifteen began to study German at home, using a periodical called 'The Popular Educator', for the purpose. He was clearly a prodigious worker, and it is difficult to imagine that any other child in the county of Dorset (or anywhere else for that matter) was better read than he!

From whence did the impetus come, that led Thomas III to drive himself so hard? From his father? Probably not, for did not the Dorset Hardys have 'all the characteristics of an old family of spent social energies', and was it not the case that Thomas III's father and grandfather 'never cared to take advantage of the many wordly opportunities' afforded them? [3.3] No, the likelihood is that the drive came from his mother, the provider of books, who insisted on him changing school in order to better himself, for she, having experienced abject poverty as a child when her mother was left destitute, had no desire to see any child of hers in the same predicament.

၄၅

Thomas III's move to Dorchester was not without its repercussions. So annoyed was Julia Martin at having her protegé removed from the school that she forthwith deprived the boy's father of all future building contracts connected with her Kingston Maurward estate. Fortunately for himself, Thomas II was able to find building contracts elsewhere, such as in helping the Earl of Ilchester repair one of his properties, Woodsford Castle, situated 5 miles to the east of Dorchester, by the River Frome.

When Thomas III contrived to see Julia Martin again, on the occasion of a harvest supper, she reproached him with having deserted her; whereupon he assured her that he had not done so, and would never do so. In fact, the sadness he felt at the enforced separation is reflected in a poem he later wrote entitled 'In Her Precincts' where, referring to Julia Martin's manor house, he wrote: 'Yes, her gloom within at the lack of me/ Seemed matching mine at the lack of her.' [3.4] It would be more than a decade before the two met again; by which time the Martins had sold their Kingston Maurward estate and moved to London.

☙

Thomas Hardy I died in 1837. In the same year, the Reverend Murray was replaced by the Reverend Arthur Shirley as Vicar of Stinsford which, for the Hardys, was no less than a catastrophe. The 'ecclesiastical changes' imposed by the new vicar now led to Thomas Hardy II abandoning in 1841 or 1842, all connection with the Stinsford string choir, in which he had played the bass viol voluntarily every Sunday for thirty-five years. The truth was that the Reverend Shirley was a vigorous reformer and innovator, who embraced the ideas of the High Church, as advocated by the three leaders of the 'Tractarian Movement' (the aim of which was to assert the authority of the Anglican Church). Nevertheless, the Hardys continued to attend church every Sunday, the 'Hardy' pew being situated in the aisle adjacent to the north wall.

Thomas III also attended the Sunday School (established by Shirley), where in due course he became an instructor, along with the vicar's two sons. In this way he gained an extensive knowledge of the Bible (Authorised Version) and the Book of Common Prayer, and was said to know the Morning and Evening services by heart, as well as the rubrics (liturgical directions), and large portions of the psalms. [3.5]

There was a great deal of antipathy on the part of Anglicans towards Catholics at the time, as evidenced when Thomas II took his son to Dorchester's Roman amphitheatre, Maumbury Rings to see an effigy of the Pope and of Cardinal Nicholas Wiseman (the first Archbishop of Westminster) being burnt during anti-Papist riots. Despite the intensity of Thomas III's Church of England upbringing, the conundrum of religion was one with which he would struggle and agonise throughout his life.

༄

Quite apart from his infatuation with Julia Martin, the lady of the manor, and hers with him, Thomas III, like many people of artistic bent, was of a deeply romantic and impressionable disposition and likely to fall in love at any moment! However, as often as not the objects of his desire were completely unaware of his attachment!

One such young lady passed him by on horseback and unaccountably smiled at him in South Walk (one of Dorchester's several tree-lined streets); another was from Windsor; a third, the pretty gamekeeper's daughter with beautiful 'bay-red' hair – she was later to be recalled in his poem 'To Lisbie Brown' – and finally there was Louisa, also recalled in 'To Louisa in the Lane'.

Hardy would also immortalise the first romantic meeting of his own parents in his poem, 'A Church Romance'.

༄

Despite the seemingly tranquil and idyllic surroundings of the Hardys' Bockhampton abode, woe betide anyone who dared to transgress against the law, or to flout the authorities, for harsh penalities awaited them! Thomas III's fascination with hanging may have been the result of his father telling him that in his day he had seen four men hanged for setting fire to a hayrick. One, a youth of eighteen, had not participated in the burnings, but had merely been present at the scene. As the youth was underfed and therefore frail, the Prison Master (governor) had ordered weights to be tied to his feet in order to be sure that his neck would be broken by the noose! 'Nothing my father ever said,' declared Thomas III, 'drove the tragedy of life so deeply into my mind.' [3.6]

24

As a youth, Thomas III was to witness two executions: the first of a woman, when he stood 'close to the gallows' at the entrance to Dorchester Gaol. [3.7] The night before he had deliberately gone down to 'hangman's cottage' situated at the bottom of the hill below the prison, beside the River Frome, and peered through the window where inside the hangman was eating a hearty supper! [3.8] The woman was Elizabeth Martha Brown, who paid the ultimate penalty for murdering her husband. 'What a fine figure she (Brown) showed against the sky as she hung in the misty rain,' wrote Thomas III later. He observed, 'how the tight, black, silk gown set off her shape as she wheeled half round and back (on the end of the rope)', indicating that perhaps the incident induced in him, not revulsion, but a measure of sexual arousal. [3.9]

The second hanging occurred one summer morning, two or three years later. Having heard that it was to take place, Thomas III took his telescope to a vantage point, focussed the instrument on Dorchester's prison and as the clock struck eight witnessed the public execution of a murderer.

4

A Career: London: Influence of Swinburne: Ill Health: Return to Dorset

Thomas III had been brought up to believe that his family was connected, albeit distantly, with other more illustrious 'Hardy' personages – past and present – in the county, such as Admiral Sir Thomas Hardy (already mentioned), his namesake, Thomas Hardy, who had endowed Dorchester's grammar school in Elizabethan times, and several others including, of course, the Channel Island Hardys, and in particular one Clement le Hardy, Baillie (chief magistrate) of Jersey. From this it may be inferred that his family were desperately anxious for the young Thomas III to succeed in the world and make something of himself, to reverse what was seen as the trend, in their case, of a family in decline.

When Thomas II was working on the Earl of Ilchester's Woodford Castle it so happened that an associate, one John Hicks, architect and church restorer, was present there with him. Thomas II duly introduced Hicks to his son, Thomas III, who also happened to be present on the day, and on the strength of this meeting, Hicks invited Thomas III to assist him in a survey. Hicks liked what he saw, and asked Thomas III to be his pupil. Thomas paid Hicks the sum of forty pounds for his son to undergo a three-year course of architectural drawing and surveying. So in 1856, when he was aged sixteen, the young Thomas started work at Hicks' office in Dorchester's South Street.

By now, Thomas III had progressed from frail and fragile childhood into vigorous manhood. His new apprenticeship did not prevent him from pursuing his reading of Latin – which enabled him to read the New Testament, Horace, Ovid, and Virgil in the original – and from teaching himself Greek, so that he could read Homer's Iliad, likewise. This necessitated him rising at five a.m. – or four in the summer months. Hicks, being a classical scholar himself, was well-disposed to Hardy's efforts in this respect.

With fellow-pupil Robert Bastow and two other youths, both recent graduates of Aberdeen University whose father was Frederick Perkins, the Baptist minister, Thomas III had furious arguments as to the merits and de-merits of 'Paedo-Baptism' (the baptism of infants). This led him to consider whether, having been baptised as an infant at Stinsford's church of St Michael, he should now be re-baptised as an adult. The question would re-surface later in Thomas III's novel, *A Laodicean*.

Next door to Hicks' office in South Street was the school of poet and philologist, Willam Barnes, who would often be called upon to adjudicate in matters of dispute in classical grammar between Thomas III and Bastow. Barnes, a Latin and Oriental scholar of great distinction, had compiled 'A Philological Grammar' in which more than sixty languages were compared.

⊙⊘

Hardy was now aged nineteen, and the year was 1859. His three-year apprenticeship was over, and he was now given the task by Hicks of making surveys of churches with a view to their 'restoration'. In reality, this was a euphemism for 'destruction', and the fact that he had once been a participant (albeit unwilling) in this process would in later years cause Thomas III enormous regret. Its legacy remains to this day, and is easily borne out by a comparison of say, the 'restored' Stinsford church of St Michael, and Puddletown's church of St Mary, which is full of magnificent and delightful historical artefacts in their original condition and situation.

The restoration of Stinsford church had begun under the aegis of the Reverend Shirley in 1843, when the main part of the west ('minstrels') gallery was removed. Shirley also removed the chancel pews, and replaced the string choir with a barrel organ! For this, the Hardy family never forgave him. Thomas III would one day get his revenge (although these traumatic events occurred when he was a mere infant), in a poem 'The Choirmaster's Burial', in which 'an unsympathetic vicar forbids William Dewey old-fashioned grave-side musical rites'. [4.1]

Thomas III was now at a crossroads; the question being whether to pursue architecture, or to immerse himself ever more deeply in the classics, and in particular the Greek plays of Aeschylus and Sophocles. In this, he was to be guided by his literary friend and mentor, Horace Moule, who had studied at both Oxford and Cambridge Universities, and had recently started as an author and reviewer. Born in 1832, he was therefore eight years senior to Thomas III. It was Moule who introduced Thomas III to the *Saturday Review*: a radical London weekly publication which attributed the majority of social evils to social inequality. He also gave Hardy books, including Johann Goethe's *Faust*.

Thomas III now commenced writing poems. His first article to be published appeared in a Dorchester newspaper, and was an anonymous account of the disappearance of the clock from the almshouse in South Street. The poem 'Domicilium' followed, together with articles published by the *Dorset Chronicle* about church restorations carried out by his employer, Hicks. Horace Moule's advice to Thomas III was, that if he wished to make his living in architecture, then he ought not to continue with his study of the Greek plays. This advice was accepted, albeit reluctantly.

෴

Why did Hardy make the decision – bold for a country youth – to go to London? Ostensibly perhaps, because he did not find working in Dorchester for Hicks challenging enough, and hoped to better himself in the capital. But in reality it may have been primarily with the object of getting a glimpse of the great writers and poets of the day, whom he wished to emulate. According to Desmond MacCarthy, an acquaintance of his, there was a more pressing reason why Hardy's thoughts had turned to writing, for he had heard that George Meredith, poet, novelist, and reader for publishers, Chapman and Hall, had received the sum of one hundred pounds for writing a novel. It was therefore Hardy's 'desire to make a little money that first made him turn to fiction.' [4.2]

In April 1862, the year of the opening of the Great Exhibition, he found temporary work making drawings for one John Norton, architect of Old Bond Street. This introduction was made by Hicks who was a friend of Norton. Soon, Norton in turn introduced Hardy to a Mr Arthur Blomfield, whom Norton had met at the Institute of British Architects. On May 5, Hardy began work as Blomfield's assistant architect.

Blomfield persuaded Hardy to sing in his own office choir, and in the choir of St Matthias' church, Richmond, where he himself sang bass. One of the duties which he assigned to his twenty-one-year-old assistant was to supervise the removal of bodies from the churchyard of Old St

28

Pancras, through which the Midland Railway company proposed to make a cutting.

That August, Hardy wrote to his sister Mary, describing how he had attended evening service at St Mary's church, Kilburn, and been visited by his friend Horace Moule who had accompanied him to a Roman Catholic chapel, built by the architect Augustus Pugin (1812-52). Two months later, Hardy wrote to Mary telling her how he and his father (who had evidently made the journey up from Dorset) had been to an opera at Covent Garden, and of how Thomas II had insisted on seeing the Thames Tunnel (from Wapping to Rotherhithe). [4.3]

This was the year in which Hardy made a proposal of marriage to Mary Waight, who was employed in the high-class 'mantle showroom' at Dorchester (retailers of women's cloaks), and at twenty-nine was seven years older than he. Mary, however, rejected his offer. [4.4]

Early in 1863, again in a letter to Mary, Hardy describes his office which overlooks the River Thames and all its bridges. However, smog, like 'brown paper or pea soup' has been a problem. He has visited the Underground Railway – then in its infancy. At the time, he was busy designing a 'Country Mansion' for a prize offered by Sir William Tite (the architect who rebuilt the Royal Exchange, and designed many of England's early railway stations) to members of the Architectural Association, of which Hardy was a member. This Hardy won. He had also entered the Prize Architectural Essay competition of the Royal Institute of British Architects (the subject being, 'The Application of Bricks and Terra Cotta to Modern Architecture'), for which he was awarded the Silver Medal. [4.5] At the end of 1863, Hardy was recommending to Mary that she read the works of William Makepiece Thackeray, whose writing he esteemed as being of the 'highest kind', and 'as a perfect and truthful representation of actual life.' He was now, in his spare time, throwing himself once more into a study of literature.

27 October, 1865 was the date of the funeral of former British Prime Minister Lord Palmerston, which Hardy was able to attend, having purchased a ticket. The following day he wrote again to Mary, commending Anthony Trollope's novel *Barchester Towers* to her as the author's best work. Hardy also mentions that his father (who is apparently staying with him at the time) has 'taken to reading newspapers'. He himself has resumed his study of French, [4.6] and was spending much time in the National Gallery studying, one at a time, the great masters,

attending a series of Shakespeare's plays, and also live readings of the works of Charles Dickens by the author himself.

෨෧

A formative influence on Hardy was the poet and writer, Algernon Charles Swinburne, born in 1837 and educated at Eton and Oxford. Swinburne's *Poems and Ballads*, published in 1865, showed a contempt for conventional morality in favour of sensuality and paganism. Although this evoked violent criticism, Hardy, who was yet to meet Swinburne, was one of his earliest admirers, and later described that, '... buoyant time of thirty years ago, when I used to read your early works walking along the crowded London streets, to my imminent risk of being knocked down'. [4.7] Swinburne's views, as expressed in his, 'Hymn of Man' – 'Glory to Man in the highest! For Man is the master of things' – would one day find an echo, in the voice of Hardy's heroine, Sue Bridehead, in his novel, *Jude the Obscure*.

෨෧

In 1866, Hardy reveals to Mary that it had been his serious intention to enter the church. Horace Moule had sent him the 'Students' Guide' to the University of Cambridge (Moule's own university), but Hardy eventually decided that his 'notion was too far fetched to be worth entertaining...'. It would take three years, and then another three, and then almost another one in order to get 'a title' (degree). [4.8] The possibility must be admitted however, that even as early as the 1860s (when he was in his twenties), when the poem 'The Incipient' is believed to have been written, he had already decided that the Christian faith was impossible to embrace. Subtitled 'At a Cathedral Service' the poem begins: 'That with this bright believing band (of worshippers)/ I have no claim to be,/ That (Those) faiths by which my comrades stand/ Seem fantasies to me...'. Also, eight years earlier, in 1858, the conflict between religion and science had been brought into sharp relief when Charles Darwin and Alfred Russell Wallace published a joint paper entitled *On the Tendency of Species to form Varieties*. The following year, *On the Origin of Species by means of Natural Selection* was published by Darwin alone. Hardy, with his voracious thirst for knowledge, would undoubtedly have fallen upon these works and read them avidly!

He now began sending poems which he had recently written, to various magazines with a view to publication, only to have them rejected by their editors.

৩৩

Whilst in London, Hardy demonstrated that his thirst for literature and music was as strong as ever, and he took every advantage of art galleries and the opera; neither of which had hitherto been available to him. Unfortunately however, his health had deteriorated, perhaps from the unhealthy air of the Metropolis (his lodgings fronted onto the River Thames, which was then little more than an open sewer); so on the advice of Blomfield, he returned, in July 1867, to Dorset. Blomfield believed that this would be for convalescence. Hardy however, had already been contacted by Hicks in Dorchester, who told him that he, Hicks, was in need of an assistant to help with church restoration work.

৩৩

Having returned in the autumn of 1867 to the house of his parents at Higher Bockhampton where he regained his strength and health, Hardy resumed his habit of walking to work to Dorchester every day. This time however, the work was of an irregular nature, and in his spare time, Hardy wrote his first novel *The Poor Man and the Lady*.

This was read by Horace Moule, now a regular contributor to the *Saturday Review*. Moule must have liked it because he furnished Hardy with a letter of introduction to publisher Alexander Macmillan, to whom Hardy sent the manuscript on 25 July the following year. Desperate to hear Macmillan's opinion, he wrote again to the publisher on 10 September, saying that he, Hardy, had it in mind to write another story, but has not the courage to do so, 'until something comes of the first.' [4.9]

Macmillan declined to publish the work. Although much of it was 'admirable', and one scene in particular was 'full of power and insight', he saw it as an excessive attack by Hardy on the upper classes, who were portrayed as 'heartless' in their dealings with the 'working classes'. These sentiments were echoed by John Morley, a friend of Macmillan to whom he had shown the work; the former did at least admit that the

31

author 'had stuff and purpose in him'. [4.10]

Unwilling to take 'no' for an answer, Hardy made a brief visit to London that December to see Macmillan personally. The answer was still the same, but Macmillan did suggest he try Frederick Chapman, of publishers Chapman and Hall. Hardy met Chapman the following day, left the work with him, and returned to Dorchester.

He revisited London in January 1869, when the reply from Chapman and Hall finally arrived. They would publish *The Poor Man and the Lady* only if Hardy guaranteed to furnish them with the sum of twenty pounds to cover any losses which the firm might incur.

By the time March came, Hardy, instead of being sent the proofs of the book for him to check as he expected, was asked by Chapman to visit London yet again. Here he met George Meredith (poet, novelist, and reader of manuscripts for Chapman and Hall), who gave Hardy his opinion: that the book would be perceived as 'socialistic', or even, 'revolutionary'. As such it would be liable to be attacked on all sides by conventional reviewers, and this might prove a handicap to Hardy in the future. Hardy should either rewrite the story, or write another novel with a more interesting plot. [4.11]

What had prompted Hardy to make this assault on the nobility and squirearchy in this fashion? He had already revealed the sensitivity of his nature in his concern for animals and their welfare; and one would naturally expect that this same concern would be shown for human beings. Also, during the time he was in London, he may have been influenced by riotous working-class demonstrations that had occurred in Hyde Park. Nearer to home, Hardy would also have been well aware of the six Dorset farm labourers – the so-called 'Tolpuddle Martyrs' – who had been sentenced in 1834 to be transported to Australia and Tasmania. Their 'crime' had been swearing an illegal oath, in an attempt to defend themselves against the progressive reduction of their wages from eight, to seven, and then to a threatened six shillings per week; an insufficient sum with which to support themselves and their starving families. He may also have been influenced by the heroic work of Horace Moule's father, the Reverend Henry Moule, who, as Vicar of Fordington, struggled to improve the lot of the poor of his parish, particularly during the cholera epidemic of 1854.

With dogged determination, Hardy in April 1869, sent the manuscript of *The Poor Man and the Lady* to Smith, Elder and Company, and in

December 1870, to Tinsley Brothers. It was rejected by the former, and the terms offered by the latter were unacceptable.

෬

John Hicks died in the winter of 1868/9. In April 1869, Hardy was asked by G.R. Crickmay, a Weymouth architect who had purchased Hicks' practice, if he would assist him in continuing with the work on church restorations with which the late Hicks had been involved. To this, Hardy agreed, and after spending the month of May working at the Dorchester office of his first employer, Hardy commenced work at Crickmay's office in Weymouth.

Hardy found lodgings in Weymouth, at 3 Wooperton Street, which provided him with some pleasant summer diversions. He enjoyed listening to the town band playing waltzes, newly composed by Johann Strauss; bathed every morning; and rowed in the bay every evening. He even joined a dancing class to learn the quadrille. By the time winter arrived Hardy, having completed the work set for him by Crickmay, chose to remain at Weymouth to start work on a new novel entitled *Desperate Remedies*. In February however, he returned home to Bockhampton, to concentrate more fully on the manuscript. Chapman and Hall's reader George Meredith, had criticised *The Poor Man and the Lady* for the weakness of its plot. Hardy therefore resolved that the plot of *Desperate Remedies* would be sensational! [4.12]

Within a week, Crickmay was in touch again, requesting that he go almost immediately to Cornwall 'to take a plan and particulars of a church I am about to rebuild there.' [4.13] This visit to the church of St Juliot, near Boscastle on Cornwall's north coast, was one which would change the life of the young Hardy dramatically.

෬

It was when he was in his late-twenties that Hardy formed an attachment to his cousin, Tryphena Sparks of Puddletown, and he went as far as to buy her a ring. Tryphena, born in 1851, was eleven years his junior.

5

St Juliot: *Desperate Remedies*: *Under the Greenwood Tree*

Hardy's journey from Weymouth to Cornwall on Monday, 7 March, 1870, involved him rising at four in the morning, catching the train at Dorchester station, and changing several times before reaching the station at Launceston. For the remaining 16 miles, he was obliged to hire a pony and trap, and by the time he arrived at St Juliot rectory, it was dark. Here, he met the lady who would one day become his wife; Emma Lavinia Gifford.

Emma, like Hardy now aged twenty-nine, was born in Plymouth. The daughter of a solicitor, and youngest but one of a family of five, she was brought up in a fine house not far from the sea front or 'Hoe'. She was educated privately, at a school run by 'dear, refined ladies of perfect manners...' [5.1], and was accustomed to mingling with 'the elite of the town'. [5.2] So how did Emma come to be living in this remote part of North Cornwall?

The Gifford family had moved from Plymouth to Bodmin (Cornwall) in 1860, and Emma's elder sister Helen had obtained a post as companion to an elderly lady at Tintagel, on the coast. Here, Helen met her husband-to-be, Caddell Holder, M.A. Oxon, Rector of St Juliot (the repair of whose church was the objective of Hardy's current visit), on the occasion of his visiting the house.

The Reverend Holder was born on the Caribbean island of Barbados, where his father was a judge. Educated at Trinity College, Oxford, he was aged sixty-seven, and therefore a great deal older than Helen; this being his second marriage, his first wife having died three years previously. When they married and Holder took his bride back to St Juliot, Emma went to live with them in the rectory. Here, she helped her sister in 'house affairs', and visited the 'parish folk'. [5.3] In her spare time, she rode her pony, Fanny, painted in watercolour, sketched, gathered wild flowers, and on Sundays played the harmonium.

St Juliot was a poor parish. Its patron lived abroad, and therefore it lacked funds. Its church, which dated from Saxon times, was in a state of dereliction: the tower being cracked to such an extent that the bells had to be removed. The pews were rotten, and ivy 'hung gaily from the roof timbers'. [5.4] Hence the need for an architect.

It so happened that the Reverend Holder was suffering an attack of gout when Hardy arrived, and as his wife was attending him, it was Emma who received Hardy. The parishioners, Emma included, had scrimped and saved to find the money for the church to be restored. Now the great day had come, and the arrival of the architect, in the shape of Hardy, caused great excitement; being something for which the parish had waited many years.

As Emma recalled, 'Scarcely any author and his wife could have had a much more romantic meeting', at this remote spot, with its 'beautiful sea-coast, the wild Atlantic Ocean rolling in, with its magnificent waves and spray'. [5.5] The evening itself was 'lovely... after a wild winter...'. [5.6] Emma recalled that Hardy 'had a beard', and wore 'a rather shabby great coat...'. A blue paper protruded from his pocket which proved to be, not a plan of the church, but the manuscript of a poem he had written! [5.7] Emma states that on his first visit to the church 'the architect ... (Hardy) stayed rather longer than first intended'. [5.8]

As for Hardy, his feelings on this occasion are summed up in his poem 'When I Set Out for Lyonesse', composed in 1870, and in particular the final verse:-

When I came back from Lyonesse
With magic in my eyes,
All marked with mute surmise
My radiance fair and fathomless,
When I came back from Lyonesse
With magic in my eyes!

('Lyonesse' – the poetical name for the County of Cornwall.)

Two days after his arrival, Hardy, accompanied by Emma and her sister, visited Boscastle (2 miles down the valley from St Juliot), Tintagel (legendary birthplace of King Arthur), and the quarries of Penpethy, to seek slate for the roofing of the church. Next day, Hardy and Emma walked unchaperoned on the clifftops! On the fourth day, Hardy returned home.

From then on Hardy visited St Juliot every few months; taking the opportunity to visit other local beauty spots with Emma, including the beautiful Valency Valley (the word believed to derive from the Cornish, 'melin-jy' meaning 'mill house').

൭

George Meredith, had demanded that Hardy's next novel should contain more of a plot and sure enough, he obliges. However, in *Desperate Remedies*, the fact that there are effectively two stories going on; first a romance and then a murder, makes not inconsiderable demands on the reader.

The story is as follows: on the death of their father (who is already a widower), Owen Graye and his younger sister, Cytherea leave the Midlands for Budmouth (Weymouth). Here they find lodgings, and Owen takes up the post of assistant to a local architect.

On an excursion by paddle steamer to Lulworth Cove, Owen misses the boat back. This enables Cytherea to become better acquainted with her brother's friend, Edward Springrove (who is head draughtsman in Owen's office), who has joined the steamer for the journey back. Edward and Cytherea fall in love; but the relationship founders when a problem arises. Edward is, in fact, already engaged to be married to his cousin.

Cytherea obtains employment as lady's maid to Miss Aldclyffe, who's Christian name also happens to be Cytherea, of Knapwater House. (Edward Springrove, who by now has become Cytherea's fiancée, lives at nearby Knapwater Park.) Miss Aldclyffe forms a deep emotional attachment to Cytherea (reminiscent of that which Julia Martin formed to Hardy – her 'Tommy' in real life).

Aeneas Manston is appointed steward at Knapwater House by Miss Aldclyffe; for reasons which only become apparent later on. He too is attracted to Cytherea. Manston is a married man; however, he becomes enraged by the taunts of his drunken wife, strikes her, and she dies instantly. He leads everyone to believe that she has perished in a fire, but in fact he has hidden her body in the oven of a disused brewhouse. Manston is now free to marry Cytherea. Cytherea, who is moved when Manston plays some 'saddening chords' on the organ, agrees to marry him, even though she does not love him. [5.9] In this way, she avoids being a burden on her brother, Owen, who is not in good health.

Suspicion is aroused that Mrs Manston is still alive so to avert speculation, Manston persuades another woman to impersonate her. However, a poem of Manston's is discovered, in which he had described the colour of his wife's eyes as 'azure', whereas his 'new' wife has eyes of deepest black!

As Manston is in the act of recovering the body of his real wife, and burying it, he is observed. He flees, only to be apprehended by Edward Springrove, as he is in the act of attempting to persuade Cytherea to run away with him. Manston is detained in the county jail, where he confesses to his crime, before hanging himself.

The plot is further complicated by the fact that Cytherea turns out to be the daughter of a man whom Miss Aldclyffe once loved. Also, when Miss Aldclyffe was aged seventeen, she was 'violated' (i.e. raped) by her cousin, a military officer. The child born as a result of this untoward event, was her present steward, Aeneas Manston.

On her death bed, Miss Aldclyffe confesses to Cytherea that the reason she appointed Manston as her steward was to bring him close to Cytherea; it being her dream that Cytherea, the daughter of the man she loved, and Manston, her own natural child, be married. Finally, all ends happily, when Cytherea marries Springrove, now a qualified architect (whose cousin to whom he was previously engaged, has now married someone else).

The predominant theme of the book appears to be that life is a labyrinth, and the 'ability to cope with its unexpected twists and turns, depends mainly on two things: the particular qualities with which one is endowed, and the experience gained in the labyrinth itself' [5.10]

In March 1870, Hardy sent the manuscript of *Desperate Remedies*, his second novel, to Macmillan; they declined to publish it (in the same way that they had previously declined to publish *The Poor Man and the Lady*). John Morley's (now editor of the *Fortnightly Review*) verdict was that, 'the story is ruined by the disgusting and absurd outrage which is the key to its mystery – the violation of a young lady at an evening party, and the subsequent birth of a child...'. In his opinion, this was 'too abominable to be tolerated as a central incident from which the action of the story is to move'. [5.11]

Notwithstanding this setback, the novel was accepted on 6 May by Tinsley Brothers; on condition that Hardy made some minor alterations, and of course completed the final chapters (of which he had hitherto sent them only a precis). These alterations were probably a toning down of the 'violation' (i.e. rape) scene. The final wording agreed for this scene was that Miss Aldclyffe, when, 'a young girl of seventeen, was cruelly betrayed by her cousin, a wild officer of six and twenty'. [5.12]

Hardy's heartache in his search for a publisher was finally at an end. What had motivated him to carry on with his writing in spite of these early rejections? Perhaps the seeds of creativity were sown in him by his having read so much of other people's work. It was therefore only natural that now he should want to write his own stories; leave his own mark on the world of English literature; get his own name into print, and after all, if they could do it, then why not he?

⚭

On 16 May, Hardy went again to London, where he assisted Blomfield and another architect, Raphael Brandon – an exponent of the English Gothic – and also spent time with Henry Moule who was also in the capital at that time. [5.13]

In August he visited Cornwall, and he and Emma enjoyed a visit to King Arthur's Castle, Tintagel. The decrepit tower and north aisle of St Juliot church was now razed to the ground, prior to its rebuilding, with Emma laying the foundation stone. [5.14] The pews, the Saxon north door, and the chancel screen were all discarded; but fortunately not before Hardy had made detailed drawings of them. [5.15] Crickmay and Hardy did however preserve many of the windows, the altar, the granite font, and the Elizabethan altar rails.

As the relationship between Hardy and Emma progressed from one of 'acquaintance' to one of 'affection' [5.16], she found him 'a perfectly new subject of study and delight', and he found a 'mine' in her (by which he meant a rich vein, rather than a weapon of war). [5.17] Subsequent visits would see the pair talking, 'much of plots, possible scenes, tales (presumably for stories), and poetry, and of his (Hardy's) own work'. In fact, Emma, who gave Hardy a lock of her hair as a keepsake to ameliorate the pain of their long separations, was helpful in making copies of his manuscripts (for publishers), researching, and suggesting possible alterations to the text.

༒

Tinsley's terms were that Hardy pay them the sum of seventy-five pounds, a great deal for a struggling architect who possessed only one hundred and twenty-three pounds in all the world! On March 25, 1871, *Desperate Remedies* was duly published, anonymously, in three volumes.[5.18] The book received excellent reviews in the *Athenaeum* and in the *Morning Post*; but it was villified by the *Spectator* magazine, which saw it as an 'idle prying into the ways of wickedness', and also objected to it being published anonymously. Moule, however, advised Hardy to ignore such criticism, and in an effort to counter them, he himself reviewed, *Desperate Remedies* in the *Saturday Review*. Unfortunately, however, there was a six-month delay before Moule's article was published.

༒

In *Under the Greenwood Tree*, which was to be his second published novel; written when he was aged thirty-one, Hardy did what many aspiring writers do; he wrote about what he knew best, in this case, his childhood. As for the names of his characters, he obtained them from a study of the tombstones in Stinsford churchyard!

The alternative title to *Under the Greenwood Tree* was *The Mellstock Quire*: 'Mellstock' being the collective name for the hamlets of Higher and Lower Bockhampton and Stinsford, and their surroundings. The 'Quire' refers to the choir of Stinsford church, both instrumental and vocal. John Morley, who had read Hardy's first novel, *The Poor Man and the Lady*, had made the comment that 'the opening pictures of Christmas Eve in the tranter's house are really of good quality'. Therefore, drawing strength from this, Hardy decided to begin his new novel with the tranter's Christmas party.

The themes of the novel are twofold: the love of Dick Dewy (an honest yeoman) for Fancy Day (a certified teacher) and the Quire's destruction, brought about by the advent of a new vicar, the Reverend Maybold. Dick proposes to Fancy and she accepts his offer. She has a momentary flirtation with Farmer Shiner; then accepts a second proposal of

The shoemaker's house, by Henry Moule. Photo: Dorset County Museum.

marriage (from the new vicar). Finally, she confesses to Maybold that she has acted hastily, and she and Dick get married amidst celebratory dances to the music of the Quire; under the greenwood tree!

Alongside this romance runs the story of the Quire, whose members number such colourful characters as the tranter, the shoemaker, and the simpleton. They have played their music since time immemorial, their previous vicar leaving them undisturbed, allowing them to participate in choosing the hymns, and never troubling them with a visit 'from year's end to year's end'. Now they have the Reverend Maybold, who never allows them 'a bit o' peace.' [5.19] When Maybold announces that the musicians are to be replaced with an organ, they see it as a catastrophe; yet resolve to fall gloriously 'with a bit of a flourish at Christmas', rather than be 'choked off quiet at no time in particular.' [5.20]

In view of the real life trauma which the Reverend Shirley had brought to the Stinsford choir, it must have given Hardy enormous pleasure and satisfaction to have Fancy Day turn down the Reverend Maybold in favour of Dick Dewy!

Hardy sent the manuscript to Macmillan, who would probably have published it, but for a misunderstanding. When the manuscript was returned to him, Hardy was of a mind to give up writing altogether; but was persuaded in a letter from Emma to persevere with it, as she felt sure this was his true vocation. In this, Emma demonstrated an unselfish side to her nature, after all, a career in architecture would have been a quicker, and more certain way for Hardy to be able to maintain her, in the event of them one day marrying one another.

๏

In the spring of 1872, Hardy returned again to London, with the aim of furthering his architectural career. He found work with a Mr T. Roger Smith, Professor of Architecture at the Royal Institute of British Architects, whom Hardy assisted in the design of schools for the London School Board.

In a chance meeting with Horace Moule, Hardy was advised to continue with his writing which, in the event of any failure of his eyesight precluding him from continuing with his architectural drawing, would provide him with an alternative occupation.

By another coincidence, Hardy encountered Tinsley, who asked him whether he had any other manuscripts for him to look at. Hardy accordingly sent Tinsley, in April 1872, the manuscript of *Under the Greenwood Tree*, which was duly published two months later, in June. The book was reviewed favourably in the *Athenaeum*, and in the, *Pall Mall Gazette*; and on the strength of this, Tinsley asked Hardy to write a story for his *Tinsley's Magazine*, to be serialised over a period of twelve months. (In Victorian times, to be published in a popular magazine could provide a lucrative source of income for an aspiring new writer.)

To this end, Hardy, in August 1872, took a break from work and commenced his next novel, *A Pair of Blue Eyes*, which was inspired by his visit to Cornwall and his meeting with Emma, two and a half years previously. Meanwhile, on April 11, 1872, the church of St Juliot was reopened, although neither Hardy nor Crickmay attended the ceremony.

In August, Hardy made another visit to Cornwall, to Kirland House, on the edge of Bodmin Town, where Emma's parents, the Giffords, were now living, having been forced to leave Plymouth due to financial difficulties. It is likely that the purpose of this visit was for Hardy to ask

Emma's father, John Attersoll Gifford, for permission to marry his daughter; strictly speaking, this was not necessary as both parties were of age (over twenty-one). Nevertheless, it was the convention of the times.

In the event, the visit was not a happy one, and this is reflected in a poem which Hardy later wrote entitled 'I Rose and Went to Rou'tor Town' ('Rou'tor' being his name for Bodmin). It appears that there was hostility from John Gifford in particular, who later referred to Hardy as 'a low-born churl who has presumed to marry into my family'. [5.21]

Emma's father's contemptuous attitude may well have reinforced Hardy's pre-existing feelings of inferiority with regard to himself. It may also have made him determined to reflect the detrimental effects of the rigid class distinctions which pervaded Victorian society (of which he was now a victim), all the more strongly in his subsequent novels.

Hardy returned to London, but quickly decided to go back to the family home at Bockhampton, in order to give *A Pair of Blue Eyes* his full attention. An invitation from Professor Smith to return to the capital was refused, despite the cordial relationship which existed between them.

6

A Pair of Blue Eyes: The Death of Moule: *Far from the Madding Crowd*

In a notebook of Hardy's are extracts from histories, biographies, but mainly from the newspaper, *The Dorset County Chronicle*, 1826-30, which demonstrate that these were his primary sources for the plots of many of his novels: for example, the 'wife-selling' scene in *The Mayor of Casterbridge*. He would borrow back numbers of the newspaper from his local library and take them home to Max Gate, where either he or Emma would make copies of anything of interest. [6.1]

However, although it seems likely that virtually everything Hardy wrote had its basis in fact, he was a master of disguise. It is therefore a brave person indeed who states with any certainty that a fictitious character from one of his novels, correlates precisely with a real life relative, friend or acquaintance of Hardy, in that he or she lived in a particular place at a particular time, and behaved in a particular way. This is because, although Hardy revealed in later years which of his fictitious 'Wessex' names he had given to this or that place (for example, 'Knollsea' – Swanage; 'Casterbridge' – Dorchester; 'Weatherbury' – Puddletown; 'Budmouth Regis' – Weymouth), [6.2] he was not averse to transposing a country mansion (also usually renamed by him) a few miles from its actual location, to suit the needs of his story, which were paramount. The same may be said of his characters. Hardy would perhaps have smiled to think what a merry dance he has led those who attempt to follow in his footsteps! This being the case, can any worthwhile deductions whatever be drawn, as to the nature of Hardy himself, from say, his third published novel, *A Pair of Blue Eyes*, where the reader is brought face to face with a drama of love, betrayal, and death; played out in the equally dramatic countryside of Cornwall? The novel was published in May, 1873, when Hardy was aged thirty-two.

The story centres around two friends who, unbeknown to one another, fall in love with the same woman. The one, Smith, is an architect who is sent to Cornwall to work on the restoration of a church. Here he meets Elfride, daughter of the parson; and falls in love. This is an exact reflection of Hardy's visit to Cornwall, when he first met Emma, his wife-to-be. Furthermore, Smith's father, like Hardy's, is a stonemason, but lives not in Dorset but not far from Elfride's home. Smith differs from Hardy however, in the fact that he travels at one point to India.

Knight, also an admirer of Elfride, is a writer, reviewer, barrister, and a former mentor of Smith; in this respect unmistakably like Horace Moule (who in 1862 was admitted to the Middle Temple). This begs the question, if 'Smith' represents Hardy, and 'Knight' represents Moule, did Moule in real life fall in love with Emma also? The answer is 'no' – in fact, Moule and Emma never met. Instead Hardy, to construct the plot, has drawn on another of his life-experiences, dating from the time when he was in love with his cousin, Tryphena Sparks. Smith's efforts to hide knowledge of his former loves from Elfride may have been a reflection of Hardy's own attempts to conceal knowledge of his former lover, Tryphena, from Emma.

怀

As always, Hardy dazzles his reader with the elegance of his writing. In *A Pair of Blue Eyes*, we discover words like 'diaphanous' (transparent), and 'parallelepipedon' (a solid figure, bounded by six parallelograms). There are delightful descriptive passages, such as when candlelight falls on Elfride, and transforms her hair 'into a nebulous haze of light, surrounding her crown like an aureola'. [6.3] He makes skilful use of imagery, for example, 'he (Smith) drew himself in with the sensitiveness of a snail'; [6.4] 'Time closed up like a fan before him (Knight)'; [6.5] '...one ray was abstracted from the glory about her (Elfride's) head'; [6.6] and 'feet', which played about under Elfride's dress 'like little mice'. [6.7]

There are references which reveal just how well read Hardy was: to authors Shakespeare and Catullus, to the Psalms, to painters Holbein and Turner, to Raphael's 'Madonna della Sedia' (depicting the Madonna and child with St John), and to 'Dundagel' (the ancient name for the Cornish village of Tintagel). Hardy reveals his attention to detail in a description of the so-called 'cliff without a name' (near 'Castle Boterel' – Boscastle); in comparison to others such as Beachy Head, St Aldhelm's, St Bee's, and the Lizard. He describes fossils known as 'Trilobites', along with their place in the history of the Earth. [6.8]

That he is in touch with the land and its people, is demonstrated when he writes of how 'labouring men' are able to tell the time of day, 'by means of shadows, winds, clouds, the movements of sheep and oxen, the singing of birds, the crowing of cocks, and a hundred other sights and sounds which people with watches in their pockets never know the existence of...'. [6.9] He is familiar with 'Hydatids', a disease of sheep, caused by tapeworm larvae, which affects the animals' brains and causes them to walk, 'round and round in a circle continually'. [6.10]

The supreme elegance of his style is shown by this description of the sea: 'And then the waves rolled in furiously – the neutral green-and-blue tongues of water slid up the slopes, and were metamorphosed into foam by a careless blow, falling back white and faint, and leaving trailing followers behind'. [6.11] He also writes knowledgeably about such places as Naples, Greece, Berlin, and even India, despite not having visited them. [6.12]

Finally, despite Hardy's reputation for unmitigated pessimism, there is much humour and wit. For example, although in English history it is a well known fact that there were only two King Charles – I and II – the driver of the cab in which Smith is travelling believes that there were more! 'Charles the Third'? – 'I really fancy that must be a mistake', replies Smith. – 'Charles the Fourth'? – 'Upon my word, that's too much'. 'Why?' answers the cab driver, after all, 'There was a George the Fourth, wasn't there?'. [6.13] And, after the death of Lady Luxellian, wife of the squire; the mourning letters had 'wonderful black rims... half-an-inch wide', was this too excessive, and was it really possible for people to feel grief to the extent of 'more than a very narrow border...' even under such sad circumstances? [6.14]

Hardy undoubtedly had a keen sense of humour; but did he ever laugh? Writer and critic Desmond MacCarthy says that he did; but that, 'his laughter made no sound. As is usual with subtle people, his voice was never loud, and a gentle eagerness, which was very pleasing, showed in his manner when he wanted sympathy about some point.' However, MacCarthy states that Hardy, 'would instantly recoil on being disappointed'. [6.15] Another acquaintance of Hardy's, Newman Flower, states that when Hardy was amused, 'A happy smile would flick across his face like a flash of summer lightning. He would inwardly chuckle: he would relate a humourous happening he had known, and rejoice in it.' [6.16]

These qualities, admirable though they are, are not sufficient to make a story. So how does Hardy craft his love triangle, so as to keep the reader interested right up until the final page – which he does. The answer lies in the character of Knight; a man animated by 'a spirit of self-denial, verging on asceticism...', [6.17] whose imagination had been 'fed... by lonely study', and whose emotions had been 'drawn out ... by his seclusion'. [6.18] (Perhaps Hardy has here added a little of himself to the mixture!) Knight's 'introspective tendencies' have 'never brought himself much happiness.' Knight's inflexibility demands that in his love for the object of his desire, Elfride, he must be 'the first-comer'. He simply cannot tolerate an 'idol' who is 'second-hand'. [6.19]

With the help of clues dropped in along the way, Knight becomes ever more suspicious that he was not, in fact, Elfride's first love; an earring, which Elfride had previously lost when in the company of Smith, and which she later rediscovers when in the company of Knight; [6.20] a tombstone – that of Elfride's fist love, Jethway, on which she once sat with her second love, Smith: [6.21] a myrtle tree, chosen in ignorance by Knight as a memento of Elfride, which was previously worn by Smith in his button hole: [6.22] and a letter from Mrs Jethway, mother of Elfride's deceased first love, in which Knight is told the full story of Elfride's previous attachments. When Knight realises that faces drawn by Smith as designs for proposed stained glass images of saints and angels, all bear a likeness to Elfride, Knight finally learns what for him is the awful truth.

The final twist-in-the-tail presents itself when Knight and Smith find themselves journeying together back from London to Cornwall; each to claim Elfride for his own; not realising that the coffin containing her dead body, is also travelling with them!

☙

As well as confirming Hardy's brilliance as a novelist, what does *A Pair of Blue Eyes* reveal about him as a person? Regarding the female sex, he says that it is a 'trick' (i.e. a skill) to read truly 'the enigmatic forces at work in women at given times'. [6.23] 'Directly domineering (of the woman) ceases in the man, snubbing (belittling of the man) begins in the woman'. And Smith had encouraged Elfride in this by 'dispraising himself' to her, which had led her to undervalue him. [6.24] Hardy's criticisms, however, were not reserved for the female sex. 'What fickle beings we men are...!', says Knight to Smith. 'Men may love strongest for a while, but women love longest'. [6.25]

Of human sensitivity, we see how mortified Elfride is by Knight's scathing review at her 'novelette'; surely a reflection of Hardy's own lack of success in his early years of writing. Of nature, he is shrewdly sanguine; she is, 'one who does not scatter kindnesses and cruelties alternately, impartially, and in order; but heartless severities or overwhelming generosities in lawless caprice.'

A great theme, which was to pervade much of Hardy's thinking and writing throughout his life, was that of social class and consequent feelings of social superiority or, in his case, inferiority. 'Fancy a man not being able to ride!', says Elfride to Smith, who sorrowfully confesses that he does not. [6.26] 'Did you ever think what my parents might be, or what society I originally moved in?' enquires Smith of Elfride, and he reveals to her that he attended a 'Dame school' originally, and then a national school. 'Well, I love you just as much...', she replies. Smith then tells her that his father is a 'cottager and working master mason'. 'That is a strange idea to me', she replies, 'but never mind, what does it matter?' [6.27]

To Elfride's father the Reverend Swancourt, however it does matter. 'He [Smith] a villager's son; and we, Swancourts, connections of the Luxellians', he cries indignantly, on discovering his daughter's attachment to Smith... What shall I next invite here, I wonder?' Why, if his daughter were to marry Smith, Elfride would always be known thereafter as 'the wife of Jack Smith the mason's son, and not under any circumstances as the wife of a London professional man (i.e. architect).' In the parson's experience, it was always the 'drawback', and 'not the compensating factor' which was talked of in society. [6.28]

The Reverend Swancourt's suspicions about Smith had been aroused on account of Smith not caring about 'sauces (i.e. relishes) of any kind'. 'I always did doubt a man's being a gentleman if his palate had no acquired tastes.' After all, was not the 'unedified palate ... the irrepressible cloven foot of the upstart?' Why, the Reverend might have brought out (i.e. wasted) a bottle of his '40 Martinez' (Portuguese wine), of which he had only eleven bottles left, on 'a man who didn't know it from eighteenpenny!' [6.29]

In those times, a person's position in the social scale; reflected in their etiquette and manners, was everything. Elfride's stepmother was obliged to rebuke Elfride for making inappropriate use of the word, 'gentlemen'. 'We have handed over 'gentlemen' to the lower middle class,' she said haughtily, 'where the word is still to be heard at tradesmen's balls and provincial tea parties.' It was now, 'Ladies and MEN', always!

⌒⌒

The first instalment of *A Pair of Blue Eyes* appeared in *Tinsley's Magazine* in September 1872, and in May 1873, the novel was published by Tinsley Brothers in three volumes.

In June, on a visit to Cambridge, Hardy met Moule, and the two of them visited Kings College Chapel, from the roof of which they could see Ely Cathedral, 'gleaming in the distant sunlight'. [6.30] (Whatever doubts Hardy may have had about the dogma of Christianity he was still in love with its ritual and imagery.) This was to be his and Moule's last encounter.

Hardy visited St Juliot on two occasions during 1873; the second time at Christmas, and this would be the last time he and Emma would go there together during all the long years of their marriage.

⌒⌒

On September 21, 1873, Horace Moule, in his rooms at Queens College, Cambridge (where he was employed as a poor law inspector) took his own life. He had befriended Hardy, encouraged him with the gift of books and intellectually stimulating conversations, set him on the road to socialism, and shielded and defended him when his own (i.e. Hardy's) books were denigrated by other critics. However, for years Moule, a taker of opium and a heavy drinker, had battled against monumental depression and suicidal tendencies. In the final analysis, Hardy's great

Horace Moule.
Photo: Dorset County Museum.

48

friend and comrade had been unable to help himself.

What was it that had brought the two of them so closely together? Perhaps in Hardy, Moule recognised a kindred spirit; a person, like himself, of great sensitivity, who saw enormous suffering in the world, and found it hard to bear.

Moule's body was brought back to Fordington for burial in consecrated ground. This was possible because, although it was normally considered a crime for a person to commit suicide, the jury had returned a verdict of 'temporary insanity'. Hardy was nonplussed and wrote, quoting Psalm 74, 'Not one is there among us that understandeth any more.'

෬৩

In December 1872, Leslie Stephen, who had been impressed with his reading of *Under the Greenwood Tree*, asked Hardy to provide a story suitable for serialisation in the *Cornhill Magazine*, of which he was editor. Stephen, a philosopher and man of letters, was also editor of the *Dictionary of National Biography*. A year later, Hardy would meet Stephen in person, and the two would become lifelong friends.

Therefore, having completed *A Pair of Blue Eyes*, Hardy set out to write *Far from the Madding Crowd*, arguably his best-loved novel. In it he ventures beyond the intimate experiences of himself and his family, (as had hitherto been the case, with the exception of *Desperate Remedies*), and instead, uses as the basis of the plot a story, told to him by his cousin Tryphena Sparks, of a woman who had inherited a farm which, contrary to the tradition of the times, she insisted upon managing herself.

The novel is set in and around Puddletown ('Weatherbury'). It is said that during the writing of it when Hardy remembered to carry a pocket notebook, 'his mind was as barren as the Sahara (desert)', yet when he did not, he was obliged to search for 'large, dead leaves', 'white chips' of wood left behind by the wood cutters, 'or pieces of stone or slate that came to hand.' [6.31]

෬৩

Gabriel Oak, known as 'Farmer Oak' on account of him leasing a sheep farm on which he keeps two hundred sheep, comes across an attractive young lady, riding in a cart. She approaches a toll gate but refuses to pay the gate-keeper his full fare. Oak makes up the difference, two-pence, but on receiving no thanks for his pains, describes her as vain.

However, he is determined to make her his wife, and to this end calls at her house with the gift of a lamb. 'I am only an every day sort of man,' he tells her, self-deprecatingly. He has a 'nice, snug little farm', and when they are married, promises to work 'twice as hard as I do now'. Immediately, music is introduced into the story. If Bathsheba Everdene, as the maiden is called, marries him, she shall have a piano 'in a year or two', and he will practise on the flute and play to her in the evenings. He will love her he says, until he dies. [6.32]

Oak's offer is refused. Bathsheba says she does not love him; throws in the fact that she is better educated than he, and advises that he find someone to provide him with the money with which to stock a larger farm. 'Then I'll ask you no more,' says Oak. [6.33] Another disaster befalls Oak when an over-zealous sheepdog chases his flock over a precipice.

Having sought employment at Casterbridge, Oak now travels in a waggon to Shottsford fair to do likewise. En route, he hears the waggoner describing a woman, evidently a farmer, who is a 'very vain feymell (female)' who can 'play the peanner (piano)'. He deduces correctly that this woman is none other than Bathsheba. The term

Sheep washing at Spring Bottom, by Henry Moule.
Photo: Dorset County Museum.

'coquettish', a woman who trifles with a man's affections, was also used by Hardy to describe Bathsheba. [6.34]

Having alighted from the waggon Oak sees a fire, and Hardy in his description of burning hayricks 'the wind blows the fire inwards, the portion in flames completely disappears like melting sugar, and the outline is lost to the eye', once more discloses his deep knowledge of country matters. [6.35] By the judicious placement of tarpaulins around the base of the stack to stop the draught, and with the application of water, Oak saves the day. His actions do not go unnoticed, and the lady-farmer (who is indeed Miss Everdene), agrees to employ him as her shepherd. A deputy is required to assist Oak; the person chosen being 'Young Cain Ball'. 'How did he come by such a name as Cain?', enquires Bathsheba. The answer was because his mother was not 'a Scripture-read woman', and believed that it was Abel who killed Cain, instead of the other way round, and therefore a mistake was made at his christening. [6.36] As always, the Bible is never far from Hardy's thoughts!

Bathsheba catches her farm bailiff stealing barley; she dismisses him, and instead of seeking a replacement, 'swears she'll do everything herself'. [6.37] At the same time, Fanny Robin, the youngest of her servants, goes missing. In fact, impatient to be married, she has gone to see her 'young man', Sergeant Troy of the militia.

Bathsheba buys a Valentine's Day card, thinking to send it to a child, but instead sends it as a prank to Farmer Boldwood, a bachelor who has a neighbouring farm. The words imprinted on its seal read 'Marry Me'. Boldwood shows the card to Oak, who tells him that the handwriting on it is Miss Everdene's.

Fanny Robin's plans to marry Troy encounter a hitch, when she mistakenly goes to the wrong church. Boldwood, who has taken the sending of the Valentine card seriously, proposes marriage to Bathsheba, who refuses on the grounds that she does not love him. She admits to him that the sending of the Valentine card was 'wanton' and 'thoughtless' on her part. [6.38] She asks Oak his opinion, and he gives it to her in no uncertain terms. The act was 'unworthy of any thoughtful, and meek, and comely woman'. [6.39] Leading a man on, whom she did not care for was 'not a praiseworthy action'. Bathsheba is incensed by Oak's criticism of her and she orders him to leave the farm. Oak is quickly recalled however, when his services are required to cure the sheep, which have become bloated and sick after breaking down the fence and getting into a field of clover.

Boldwood reappears at the (sheep) shearing supper, where there is much music and merriment. 'I be in liquor, and the gift is wanting in me,' says Joseph Poorgrass when he is asked to sing. He nonetheless obliges! One night, Bathsheba is taking a final look around the farm when she encounters Sergeant Troy. Her skirt becomes entangled in his riding spur. 'I wish it had been the knot of knots, which there's no untying,' he says, on catching sight of her beautiful face. Troy had told Bathsheba she was beautiful; Farmer Boldwood never had, and this she regarded as a a fatal omission on Boldwood's part!

Bathsheba meets Troy again at the haymaking, where he is assisting. He gives her a gold watch which had belonged to his father. He then helps her with her bees, and gives her an exhibition of sword play. Here, Hardy, in describing the various 'infantry cuts and guards', shows again his attention to detail.

Despite being warned of the danger by Oak, who she once again dismisses from the farm, Bathsheba confesses to her maid Liddy, that she loves Troy, 'to very distraction and agony'. When Boldwood discovers this he is distraught. Bathsheba now decides to travel to Bath, where Troy is currently staying, and 'bid him farewell'. [6.40] Troy, on his return, encounters Boldwood, who encourages him to marry Fanny Robin. However, when Boldwood sees how much Bathsheba appears to love Troy, he changes his mind and exhorts Troy instead to marry Bathsheba. Troy then informs Boldwood that he (Troy) and Bathsheba had recently married in Bath.

At the harvest supper and dance, when all the employees are the worse for drink, a storm blows up but Oak, with Bathsheba's help, manages to save the precious hayricks once again. Bathsheba confesses to Oak that, when she visited Troy in Bath, he had emotionally blackmailed her, by saying that he had seen a woman more beautiful than her, and therefore could not be counted upon unless she, 'at once became his'. Therefore, through 'jealousy and distraction', she married him. [6.41]

Troy demands money from Bathsheba for gambling purposes. She becomes suspicious when they encounter a poor woman en route to the Casterbridge Union-house (workhouse), whom Troy appears to know. It is Fanny Robin. Troy promises to meet her and bring her money in two days time. He confesses to Bathsheba that this is the woman he was intending to marry before he met her. Bathsheba realises that her romance with Troy has come to an end. When news comes that

Fanny Robin has died, Bathsheba sends a waggon to Casterbridge to collect her coffin.

On the return journey with the coffin, driver Joseph Poorgrass, who 'felt anything but cheerful' and wished he had some company, calls in at an inn, where Oak finds him so drunk that he himself (Oak) is obliged to drive the waggon for the remainder of its journey. Poorgrass denies it; 'All that's the matter with me' he says, 'is the affliction called a multiplying eye.' [6.42]. This is Hardy's rustic humour at its best! However, it is now too late for the funeral to take place, so this is postponed until the following day. Meanwhile, the coffin is kept at Bathsheba's house in a sitting-room next to the hall.

While awaiting her husband's return, Bathsheba, suspecting that Fanny Robin has had a baby, allows her curiosity to overcome her. She prises open the coffin lid, and her worst fears are realised; there are in fact, two bodies inside, one of an infant child. Troy returns, sees the situation, kisses the corpse and tells Bathsheba, 'This woman is more to me, dead as she is, than ever you were, or are, or can be.'

Troy, miserable after the death of Fanny Robin, choses to disappear from the scene and Bathsheba believes him to be dead; he having left his clothes on a beach prior to going for a swim from which he did not return. However, in reality he has found employment at a sheep fair, in an 'entertainment' (performance) where he takes the part of highwayman, Dick Turpin.

Boldwood finally extracts from a most reluctant Bathsheba, a promise that she will marry him in six years time, provided that Troy has not returned. However, Troy does return, making himself known at a party held by Boldwood one Chrismas Eve. He summons Bathsheba, who is present, seizes her arm, and Boldwood shoots him dead.

Oak, meanwhile, has decided to emigrate to California. Bathsheba is dismayed at this news; the wheel has turned full circle, and now it is she who wants him! This causes Oak to change his mind, and move instead to a small farm in the locality. Would Bathsheba allow him to love her, win her, and marry her (even though, as he puts it, 'I've danced at your skittish heels ... for many a long mile, and many a long day...'). 'But you will never know,' she replies. 'Why?' 'Because you never ask.'

෬෨

In *Far from the Madding Crowd*, which Leslie Stephen helped him to edit, Hardy is at his brilliant best. He has just had the honour, and is experiencing the joy, of being asked by a publisher for a manuscript, rather than as previously, having to endure the painful process of seeking one out. Now, confidently and without inhibition, he is able to paint brilliantly in a firmament of colour, the life and landscape of his beloved Wessex; the backdrop of this romantic story where steadfastness, personified by Oak, and coquettishness, by Bathsheba, find themselves in juxtaposition. Finally, after a scintillating admixture of humour and tragedy, there is a resolution; and the couple marry to the sound of cannon fire and numerous musical instruments including drum, tambourine, serpent, tenor viol and double bass. [6.43]

Far from the Madding Crowd was serialised between January and December 1874; and on the strength of Hardy having been paid the sum of four hundred pounds by *Cornhill's* publishers Smith, Elder and Co., he and Emma could now afford to marry.

7

Marriage: Swanage and *The Hand of Ethelberta*: The Continent: Sturminster Newton: *The Return of the Native*

Hardy and Emma were married on September 17, 1874. Hardy was living in lodgings at Westbourne Park, Paddington at the time, and the couple were married in the local church of St Peter. Emma's uncle Dr E. Hamilton Gifford, Canon of Worcester cathedral, officiated; the only other people present being Emma's brother Walter Gifford (born 1847), a civil servant, and Sarah Williams, the daughter of Hardy's landlady, who signed the register as a witness. [7.1]

This is curious because it was then, and is still now, common practice for a bride-to-be to be married in her own parish (Emma's parents were now living in Bodmin). Alternatively, had Emma's brother-in-law the Reverend Holder married them, then his church of St Juliot was near enough to Bodmin for Emma's parents to have attended the ceremony without difficulty.

The absence from the wedding ceremony of Hardy's parents is also noteworthy (after all, his father Thomas II was well used to visiting his son in London), as is the absence of his sisters; Mary in particular to whom he was closest, and of his brother, Henry. Could it be that the antipathy to the couple's union was not just from the Giffords? Hardy's mother Jemima, had gone to great lengths to educate her son, now an aspiring and talented young architect living in London, and she might reasonably have expected him to avail himself of all the opportunities that the capital had to offer in terms of social intercourse. Now he was throwing himself away on a nonentity of a girl from rural Cornwall, who was actively undermining her (Jemima's) efforts by encouraging her son to give up his chosen career, and embark on the much more uncertain and precarious one of attempting to become a writer. With the benefit of hindsight, it is possible to state that it was Emma who was the main obstacle to Hardy's family, whom she regarded as highly inferior to herself, attending the wedding. However, it is a measure of Emma's love for Hardy, and of his for her that, despite all opposition and reservations, they still went ahead with the marriage.

After a few days at the Palace Hotel, Queensway, and then at Brighton, the couple spent their honeymoon (September-October 1874) in Rouen, Paris and Versailles, where Hardy hoped to collect material for his next story.

In Paris they visited Notre Dame cathedral, the Louvre Museum, and the Tuileries Gardens (all that remained of the seventeenth-century Tuileries Palace, which was destroyed in 1871). Emma made some rather contemptuous comments about the Parisian 'working classes' who were, 'very short and small altogether – pigmies in fact – men and women – the old women very ugly and dark.' These remarks were not at all in keeping with Hardy's sentiments, which were always to champion the cause of such people. There is little sentiment in Emma Hardy's diary of events, but much detailed description of bedrooms, streets, children, domestic animals, and in particular, hotel menus! [7.2]

Emma Lavinia Hardy.
Photo: Dorset County Museum.

For Hardy, ever intrigued by the macabre, no visit to Paris would be complete without him seeing the city mortuary (La Morgue), where according to Emma, they saw 'Three bodies – (the) middle one pink – their clothes hanging above them.' She found the experience 'Not offensive, but repulsive', which was not surprising, as this was supposed to be her honeymoon! [7.3] They returned to England on October 1; Emma recording in her Diary, 'Dirty London. Very wet.'

They found lodgings for a time in Surbiton from where Hardy wrote to novelist Katherine Macquoid, giving his views on 'whether women of ordinary types should or should not be depicted as the heroines of novels...'. Women were 'quite worthy enough in nature', yes, he said, but all too frequently they did not 'exhibit that nature true and simply...'.

Bathsheba, he considered, 'was not devoid of honesty of this kind', and 'no satire on the (female) sex' was intended by the imperfections of his heroines. He, Hardy, was more concerned in his art with 'picturesqueness', than with 'perfect symmetry'. [7.4] One day Emma's father, John Gifford arrived at their home unexpectedly, which was curious considering that he had not attended their wedding. Emma mentioned the visit in her diary, but gave no explanation for it. [7.5] The couple then transferred to Hardy's former lodgings at Westbourne Grove, Paddington.

Meanwhile, public demand for *Far from the Madding Crowd* was so great that its publishers Smith, Elder and Co. requested that Hardy write them another story.

⊙◯

Hardy was still living in London when he commenced the writing of *The Hand of Ethelberta – A Comedy in Chapters*, in which figured recently visited Rouen and Paris. However, as a person who loved solitude, he was beginning to find living in the capital a strain. It was difficult to accept the advice given to him by Anne, daughter of novelist William Thackeray (and sister-in-law of Leslie Stephen), that 'a novelist must necessarily like society'. His first novel *The Poor Man and the Lady*, had been rejected on the grounds that it portrayed the upper classes as being uniformly bad. He now decided to write a light-hearted satirical comedy about them.

When, early in 1875, Hardy sent to his publisher the introductory chapters of his new novel, the immediate reaction was that this was no comedy' in the accepted sense of the word, and he was advised to abandon the subtitle. In May, he (Hardy) wrote to Leslie Stephen, agreeing with this proposal and explaining his purpose in writing the novel. The story, he said, 'would concern the follies of life, rather than the passions...'. He would tell it 'in something of a comedy form; all the people having weaknesses at which the superior lookers-on smile, instead of being ideal characters'. [7.6]

In the book's preface he went into more detail. Describing the narrative as 'somewhat frivolous', he said he had undertaken the 'delicate task' of exciting 'interest in a drama' in which 'servants were as important as, or more important than, their masters...'. He had reversed the 'social foreground' so that the 'drawing room was sketched (portrayed) in many cases from the point of view of the servants' hall.' [7.7]

⟲

In March 1875, Leslie Stephen, who had long since taken over from the late Horace Moule as Hardy's mentor and confidant, summoned him to witness his signature on a deed. Stephen, once a Fellow and Tutor of Trinity Hall, Cambridge, had been ordained with a view to becoming a parson. However, in 1862, because of a loss of faith, he had resigned his tutorship and moved to London. Now he informed Hardy that he had belatedly decided to renounce Holy Orders.

He told Hardy that he had 'wasted' too much time on religion and metaphysics, and instead had become fascinated by the new theory of 'vortex rings'. [7.8] This was a reference to the views of Francois Comte (the French philosopher and mathematician), who advocated 'humanism', believing that man had passed through the theological phase to that of the 'Positive' in which science had taken the place of theology and philosophy. Hardy too, had made a study of the works of Comte, and this renunciation of faith by Stephen, his dearest friend, would undoubtedly have led Hardy to question his own religious beliefs.

⟲

On July 12, 1875, Emma Hardy recorded in her diary, 'Left London for Bournemouth'. Three days later she and Hardy were in Swanage, where they found lodgings at West End Cottage, on the east side of the town, adjacent to the downs and overlooking Swanage Bay. This would be the first of many sojourns the couple would make in various locations in Dorset.

The cottage belonged to Joseph Masters, a former sea captain, who was now an invalid; he regaled them with his fascinating sea stories. Hardy continued with the writing of *The Hand of Ethelberta*, while Emma sketched boats, bathing machines and a cliff stone quarry. She described a trip by 'steamer' (boat) to the Isle of Wight, and a picnic at Corfe Castle, where she and Hardy were joined by his sisters Mary and Katharine, and by his brother Henry – 'A splendid day'. [7.9]

The Keep, Corfe Castle, by Henry Moule.
Photo: Dorset County Museum.

Any tensions between the two families for the younger generation at least, appear to have been resolved.

⟨൭⟩

The heroine of the story, Ethelberta Chickerel, is the daughter of a butler; she hopes that publishing some poems she has written will enable her to support her brothers and sisters, and her infirm mother. In this she is disappointed. Ethelberta is a free spirit whose aim is to enter an intellectual society, and at the same time pursue her writing. This she can achieve by marrying a man of means, who will permit her to do this.

She marries, first the son of the gentleman of the house in which she is employed as a governess, but he dies, leaving her a widow at the age of twenty-one. Her objective now is to retain her position in society which she does by concealing her lowly origins and marrying Lord Mountclere. Although she becomes a successful author, nevertheless she dislikes the trumpeting of 'drawing room' success, as much as Hardy himself does in real life.

When she brings her brothers Dan and Sol, who are builders, up from the country to her London home, Sol chastises her for 'creeping up among the useless lumber of our nation that'll be the first to burn if there comes to a flare'. Surely this is a reflection of Hardy's own views, and its strength of feeling demonstrates that his fiery indignation at the upper classes, as portrayed in his first (unpublished) novel, has by no means been quenched. Despite the presence of her brothers, Ethelberta in her new position finds herself estranged from her own kith and kin, and feels disloyal to them on this account. Ethelberta appears to be articulating Hardy's own longstanding dilemma, viz. how was it possible for a person to migrate from one social class to a higher one?

This is also a story about 'town' versus 'country'; written by a person, Hardy, who has himself discarded London in favour of rural Dorset, and there is no doubt which of the two he finds the more amenable. In his experience, country people are more loyal, honest, generous, and colourful; as well as being healthier.

⟨൭⟩

In March 1875, George Smith, head of Smith, Elder & Co., accepted *The*

Hand of Ethelberta for serialisation in the Cornhill magazine. For Hardy, the work represented a complete departure from what he had previously written. He admitted that the 'migratory circumstances' of the novel (i.e. the many different places in which the action was set) 'were deemed eccentric' on its first publication. [7.10] This was not one of the most successful of his novels; so what had persuaded him to depart from a winning formula and 'forsake the farm for the drawing room'? According to Hardy's American acquaintance and admirer, Rebekah Owen, this was because of the adverse criticism that *Far from the Madding Crowd* had received. [7.11] It seemed therefore, that of all Hardy's talents, writing satire was not one of them! By the time *The Hand of Ethelberta* was published in April 1876, Hardy and Emma had moved to lodgings in Yeovil while they sought more permanent accommodation.

࿘

In May 1876, from their lodgings in Yeovil, Hardy and Emma travelled once again to the continent, to visit Holland and Germany. Here, the cathedrals of Cologne and Mainz proved of great interest to the thirty-six-year-old architect-turned-writer, and as for Emma, her diary records that she paid great attention to the religious paintings of the 'masters' in the 'Picture Gallery at Antwerp', and to the religious iconography on display in the local churches. [7.12]

࿘

On July 3, 1876, the couple found lodgings at 'Riverside Villa' which overlooked the River Stour at Sturminster Newton, where they remained for almost two years. Here, Hardy wrote poems and allowed his fertile imagination to be fed with the local legends, superstitions and folklore of the region; his fund, of course, for further stories! That Christmas of 1876/7, they stayed at Bockhampton, and this appears be the first time that Hardy's parents met Emma.

In October 1877, Hardy visited Bath, where he obtained lodgings for his father Thomas II, who came up from Dorchester on the train. They went to the theatre and Thomas II 'took the waters', which they both hoped would alleviate the rheumatic condition from which he was suffering.

On Coronation Day (celebrating the coronation of Queen Victoria thirty-nine years previously, on June 28, 1838), there was a holiday, with games and dancing. That December, true to form, Hardy accompanied the local coroner to an inquest on a boy who was believed to have been poisoned. This proved not to have been the case! The couple's hopes for a child were unfulfilled; a fact made more poignant when they discovered that their former maidservant, who had eloped with her lover, had herself become pregnant.

Most importantly, it was at Sturminster Newton that Hardy wrote his next novel *The Return of the Native*, set on the great and mysterious 'Egdon Heath', to the east of his home at Bockhampton.

❧

The story concerns Eustachia Vye, a nineteen-year-old who lives with her grandfather on the heath which, she says, is, 'my cross, my shame, and will be my death'. [7.13] Her desire is, 'To be loved to madness...' and only this will 'drive away the eating loneliness of her days'. [7.14]

Eustachia has formed a romantic attachment to Damon Wildeve, a failed engineer who is now an innkeeper. Wildeve, however, has agreed to marry Thomasin Yeobright, who lives with her aunt, and does so after the reddleman (who deals in red ochre, a pigment used by farmers in preparing sheep for market), Diggory Venn, intervenes to persuade Eustachia to relinquish her hold on Wildeve. (Venn was formerly a rejected suitor of Thomasin.)

Mrs Yeobright's son, Clym, now returns from Paris where he has been in the employment of a diamond merchant. Dissatisfied with this work, he proposes to give it up in favour of a more worthy occupation; that of becoming 'a schoolmaster to the poor and ignorant' at 'Budmouth' (Weymouth), 'to teach them what nobody else will'. [7.15]

Eustachia has designs on Clym whom she sees as a future husband, but perhaps more importantly, as a passport to a more romantic life. 'To be your wife and live in Paris would be heaven to me,' she says. [7.16] Clym's mother disapproves of her son abandoning his career to become a teacher, and also of his growing attachment to Eustachia, who is commonly believed to be a witch.

Clym leaves home; he and Eustachia marry, and he embarks on a course of study. He and his mother are now estranged. Clym begins to suffer from failing eyesight, which necessitates him abandoning any idea of teaching, and forces him to become a humble cutter of furze (gorse for fuel). For Eustachia, this means the end of any dream she might have had of escaping from the boredom of the heath.

One day Wildeve, who although now a married man has by no means abandoned his attachment to Eustachia, calls on her at her house. Clym is asleep, and therefore unaware of his presence. Clym's mother has decided to seek a reconciliation with her son. She visits the house and knocks at the door, but Clym does not awaken, and Eustachia chooses not to answer it. On the way home, Mrs Yeobright is bitten by an adder and dies, but before she does so, she tells a small boy Johnny Nunsuch, that she is 'a broken-hearted woman, cast off by her son'. [7.17]

Eustachia tries to conceal the truth about what has happened, but Clym finds out and Eustachia returns to her grandfather. After a period, Clym writes a letter to Eustachia proposing that they reunite but it arrives too late. Eustachia has already fled with Wildeve. Wildeve is drowned while attempting to rescue her from a stream near to a weir, but Clym and reddleman Venn, both of whom are involved in the attempted rescue, survive. Finally, Thomasin marries Diggory Venn, the faithful reddleman who has watched patiently all along, as events unfolded.

Hardy adds colour, with evocative descriptions of the heath and Rainbarrow (the ancient tumulus which contains the graves of the ancestors), with the inevitable chorus of rustic musicians, and with allusions to witchcraft, as when Eustachia is stabbed with a needle by Susan Nunsuch on the occasion of Thomasin's wedding, and the 'mummers' (play-actors), who from time immemorial have re-enacted epic plays like *St. George*, featuring such characters as 'The Turkish Knight', 'The Doctor' and 'The Valiant Soldier' for the amusement of the local populace!

∞

A criticism made of *The Return of the Native* was that its heroine Eustachia's primary aim in life appeared to be to gratify her sensual passions. This is true, and her failure to do so is what makes the story. However, there is another aspect to it. The question arises whether Hardy had his own mother in mind when he created the character of Clym's mother, Mrs Yeobright? Could it be that, like Mrs Yeobright's attitude to Eustachia (whom she describes as 'lazy and dissatisfied', [7.18] Jemima Hardy had felt that her son's chosen love Emma, a nonentity of a girl from remote Cornwall, was unworthy of marrying her son, who she hoped was just beginning to make his way in London? And had not Emma encouraged Hardy to continue with the chancy business of writing, rather than to pursue a safer and more certain career in architecture?

Could this be the reason why Jemima had avoided meeting Emma, and had failed to attend the couple's wedding? Did Hardy hope desperately for a reconciliation before his mother died, just as Mrs Yeobright had died before a reconciliation with her son Clym, and with his wife Eustachia, could be achieved? Perhaps, if there had been ill-feeling between Hardy and Emma on the one hand, and Hardy's parents on the other, a reconciliation did occur when the couple stayed at Bockhampton with Jemima and Thomas II over the Christmas of 1876/7, or perhaps it did not?

Also in the novel, we have an intimation of Hardy's abandonment of the Christian faith. Clym had 'found his vocation in the career of an itinerant open-air preacher and lecturer on morally unimpeachable subjects...'. In fact, the word preacher is misleading because 'He left alone creeds and systems of philosophy, finding enough and more than enough to occupy his tongue in the opinions and actions common to all good men'. [7.19]

By early 1878, Hardy had come to the conclusion that in order to succeed as a writer, it was necessary for him to live in or near London, and for this reason, on March 22 of that year, the couple relocated to the capital. On November 4, *The Return of the Native* was published by Smith, Elder & Co.

The Trumpet Major: A Laodicean: Illness: Wimborne: Two on a Tower

Now lodging with Emma in Upper Tooting, London, Hardy immersed himself once more in the life and culture of the capital. He was elected to the Rabelais Club (which held literary dinners every two months), and also to the exclusive Savile Club for gentlemen. Time was spent at the Grosvenor Gallery, studying and admiring sculptures and paintings. He also witnessed the final performance of actor Henry Irving, in a scene from Shakespeare's *Richard II*, at the Lyceum Theatre. Hardy's love of the theatre may have had its origins in the strolling players, whom he saw in and around Dorchester when he was a boy.

Hardy kept in touch with his native Dorset, where, in August and September of 1878, he renewed his acquaintance with poet William Barnes, and with Charles W. Moule, brother of the late Horace.

In February 1879, he was again in Dorset on a cold winter's day when his brother, Henry, met him from the railway station. It was on this occasion that his father Thomas II, informed him that when he, Thomas II, was a boy, and there was a hanging at Dorchester Prison, it was always carried out at 1p.m., in case the incoming mail-coach brought with it a reprieve of sentence! Another piece of information he gleaned was that the notorious hangman, Jack Ketch, used to perform public whippings by the town's water pump, using the cat-of-ninetails.

Back in London, Hardy attended musical soirées and literary congresses. On a visit to Harrow School he was moved by the 'little tablets', in memory of the boys who had died there; after all, this was the age of virulent infectious diseases and no antibiotics. [8.1]

Any antipathy which might have existed between Emma and Hardy on the one hand, and Hardy's parents on the other, appears to have been resolved by August 1879, because the couple visited Bockhampton, and when they stayed for a time in Weymouth, Hardy's mother visited them and accompanied them on a drive to Portland.

Once again in London, Hardy was now moving in the upper echelons of society. Among the people he met were Sir Percy Shelley, son of the poet Percy Bysshe Shelley; the poet, educationalist and writer Matthew Arnold; the poet Robert Browning; and the Poet-Laureate Lord Tennyson (who told him that of Hardy's novels he liked *A Pair of Blue Eyes* best); novelist and cartoonist George Du Maurier; and painter Sir Lawrence Alma-Tadema. He also went to the Epsom races for Derby Day.

৩৩

Hardy had been fascinated by the Napoleonic Wars ever since his boyhood, when he had discovered a magazine on the subject at his home in Bockhampton. He would also have been aware that his grandfather Thomas I, as a volunteer militiaman, had travelled with his regiment to Weymouth, to prepare for the threatened invasion by Emperor Napoleon I of France.

Back in June 1875, (the 18th of that month being Waterloo Day, commemorating the Duke of Wellington's victory over Napoleon), he and Emma had visited Chelsea Hospital and heard real-life accounts of the battle from men who had fought in it. On another excursion to the continent with Emma in 1876, he had visited Waterloo and explored the battlefield. And of course, nearer to home, he would often have seen the local 'redcoats', based at their barracks in Dorchester, exercising their horses on the downs.

Hardy availed himself of any opportunity to immerse himself in matters Napoleonic, as when he attended the funeral of the exiled Prince Louis Napoleon (only son of Emperor Napoleon III), who had been killed while fighting for Britain in the Zulu War. The Prince's body was duly brought back to England for burial at Chislehurst in Kent.

It therefore seemed inevitable that Hardy would write a novel set in this period of history, and he accordingly visited the British Museum and read C.H. Gifford's *History of the Napoleonic Wars* to acquaint himself with the full facts. Relevant material was also to be found in parish records and on local tombstones.

The Trumpet Major is set in those anxious times when an invasion of England by the forces of Napoleon seemed imminent. The story is about two brothers, John Loveday (the Trumpet Major), and Robert, a sailor. The brothers, sons of the miller, are rivals for the hand of village beauty Anne Garland. Anne vacillates as to which one she really loves, and finally it is the less deserving Robert whom she chooses; while John, reliable and self-sacrificing, sails under Admiral Lord Nelson and Captain Hardy (Thomas Hardy's ancestor), in the warship *Victory*, only to meet his death in Spain in the Peninsular War.

Included in the story is the visit of King George III to Weymouth, amidst a fanfare provided by the 'Quire' of fiddlers, violoncellists, trombonists and drummers. There is also a description of the local Dorchester 'strong beer'; a subject always close to Hardy's heart! 'It was of the most beautiful colour that the eye of an artist in beer could desire; full in body, yet brisk as a volcano: piquant, yet without a twang; luminous as an autumn sunset; free from streakiness of taste; but finally, rather heady'. [8.2]

⌖

On February 11, 1880, Hardy wrote to the Reverend Handley Moule, at that time Fellow of Trinity College, Cambridge, (who was the brother of his dear friend, the late Horace), concerning the recent death of their father, the Reverend Henry Moule, Vicar of Fordington. Hardy for many years had regarded himself as a parishioner of Henry Moule (even though 'topographically' speaking this was not the case), and he referred to the 'energies' which the vicar had brought 'to bear upon the village...'; here, Hardy would have been especially remembering Henry Moule's heroic efforts during the cholera epidemics of 1849 and 1854.

⌖

Hardy stated that of all his novels, *The Trumpet Major* was the one 'founded more largely on testimony, oral and written, than any other...'. [8.3] It was published by Smith, Elder & Co. on October 26, 1880.

⌖

In November 1880, on a visit to Cambridge, Hardy attended the 5p.m. service at Kings College Chapel. It was in Cambridge that he fell ill. On his return to London, a surgeon was summoned to determine why Hardy was experiencing acute abdominal pain. The diagnosis was that he was bleeding internally. By now, Hardy had already written the early chapters of his next novel, *A Laodicean*, to be serialised in *Harper's*

Magazine with illustrations by George Du Maurier. He was now, on account of his illness, 'forced to lie in bed with his feet higher than his head for several months'. [8.4] Therefore, the only way for him to complete his manuscript was for him to dictate it to Emma, who was also nursing him. The process began in November 1880, and was finished on May 1, 1881, by which time Hardy was able to leave his sick bed and venture outdoors once again.

Due to his illness, he and Emma had been obliged to ask for an extension to the lease of their house in Upper Tooting. Having previously been torn between London and Dorset, they now decided to return to the country. In future, they would visit the capital for a few months only each year; this they hoped would be beneficial for Hardy's health, and also provide inspiration for him in his future writing. Accordingly, they found a house in Wimborne, Dorset, named 'Llanherne'. In retrospect, it seems likely that Hardy was suffering from biliary colic, where a small stone becomes temporarily impacted in the duct which drains bile from the liver into the gut. This would account for his jaundice, as observed by Edmund Gosse who was visiting at the time. [8.5] Renal colic, again caused by a stone, is another possibility. However, this might well have manifested itself by haematuria (blood in the urine), or by Hardy actually passing the stone, of which there is no mention.

☙

In July 1881, Hardy and Emma, in company with Hardy's younger sister Katharine, visited the ancient British stronghold of Badbury Rings, and Kingston Lacy (seat of the Bankes family). Hardy also pointed out on the journey, Charborough, the home of Mrs Drax (noted for the tall tower which stood in its grounds). [8.6] In August 1881, the couple travelled extensively in Scotland, where they visited castles and lochs, and Hardy sketched. On their return, they attended a ball given by Lady Wimborne at Canford Manor.

☙

Hardy presumably derived the name of the novel, *A Laodicean*, from the Bible's book of Revelations, 'lukewarm in religion, like the Christians of

Laodicea', [8.7] and the description applies equally well to the heroine of the story, Paula Power.

Paula's father purchases a castle from the ancient 'De Stancy' family, one of whose members Charlotte, who is now penniless, continues to live there as a friend of Paula. The hero George Somerset is, like Hardy, an architect, music lover and poet. He has a jealous rival for Paula's hand in the envious James Havill, also an architect. Other characters include Captain William de Stancy, Charlotte's brother, who hopes to marry Paula and thereby reclaim the ancestral home, and William Dare, De Stancy's illegitimate son.

Paula adores the 'romantic and historical'; thinks the castle wonderful, and even wishes that she was one of the ancient 'De Stancy' family who had built it all those years ago. However, whereas William de Stancy can offer Paula pedigree, and a title to go with it, Somerset reminds Paula that there is another nobility, one of 'talent and enterprise', and he cites such notable people from the past as Archimedes, Newcomen, Watt, Telford and Stephenson. In fact, Paula's father is himself an engineer and builder of railways. Finally, it is George who wins the day and he and Paula become man and wife.

In Hardy's own words, *A Laodicean* contained 'more of the facts of his own life than anything else he had ever written'. [8.8] Certainly, when he first met Emma at St Juliot, there was a rival already in existence there, namely one Henry Jose, a twenty-five-year-old farmer and churchwarden. The novel shows that far from being entrenched in the past, Hardy was quite willing to recognise and embrace the advances of science, as long as the effect was not to enslave the people or destroy the landscape – viz. threshing and ploughing machines driven by steam traction engines. An 'old chestnut', the subject of Infant Baptism, is revived, and minister 'Mr Woodwell' in the novel is clearly based on Frederick Perkins of Dorchester; the Baptist minister, and father of the two youths with whom Hardy used to have deep discussions on the subject.

A Laodicean, which appeared in *Harper's Magazine* between December 1880 and December 1881, was published in December 1881 by Sampson Low of London.

☙

On April 26, 1882, during a stay in London, Hardy attended the funeral of Charles Darwin, whose book *The Origin of Species* he had long admired, and which had posed serious philosophical questions for him when he had first read it many years previously. On May 13, he described the 'slow, meditative lives of people who live in habitual solitude...', a condition which 'renders every trivial act ... full of interest'. [8.9]

In September, on a journey which took him to three counties, he demonstrated his concern for animals in a description of a journey from Axminster in Devon to Lyme Regis in Dorset. 'The horse (pulling the coach) swayed...' and 'leant against the pole'. His head 'hung like his tail. The straps and brass rings of the harness seemed barbarously harsh on his shrinking skin.' Emma would apparently have intervened, had it not been for the 'anger of the other passengers, who wanted to get on (with the journey)'. [8.10] In early October, Hardy and Emma set out once more for France, where they explored Paris and visited the Louvre Art Gallery and the Luxembourg Museums of Art.

The Reverend Holder, Rector of St Juliot, and husband of Emma's sister Helen, died in the November. He had apparently been on friendly terms with Hardy, whom he had regaled with many an amusing story, and whom he had permitted to read the lesson at church services, when he himself had been 'not in vigour'! [8.11]

In May and June 1883, the couple made their customary visit to London, where Hardy once again met Robert Browning.

The novel *Two on a Tower* was to be about astronomy, and as so often with Hardy, beneath the superficial story was a great theme. This time the theme, which he described in the Preface was 'the outcome of a wish (of his) to set the emotional history of two infinitesimal lives against the stupendous background of the stellar universe'.

To achieve this, it was necessary for Hardy to obtain permission to visit the Greenwich Observatory from the Astronomer Royal. Hardy required an answer to the following question. Was it possible to site a telescope with which to study the stars in an old tower, despite the fact that it had not been built for the purpose? In his mind was the great eighteenth-century tower, which stood in the grounds of Charborough Park near Wimborne. The aristocratic Lady Viviette Constantine, believing herself to be a widow, falls in love with Swithin St. Cleeve, a curate's son, who is considerably younger than she is. She provides him with astronomical instruments, and sets him up in a tower on her estate, which he uses as an observatory. Having married Swithin, she then discovers that her 'late' husband, Sir Blount (who she was told had died of a fever in South Africa), is still alive. She is now pregnant, and anxious not to be a burden on Swithin, or to impede his progress as an architect, she cancels her marriage to him and, to gain respectability for herself, proceeds to marry the Bishop of Melchester. In constructing the character of Lady Constantine it is possible that Hardy had in mind Julia Martin of Kingston Maurward, who had adopted him as her protégé, and as her own surrogate child. *Two on a Tower* was published by Sampson Low in late October 1882.

☙

In 1883, an article entitled 'The Dorsetshire Labourer', written by Hardy, was published in *Longman's Magazine*. Such a person was hitherto personified as having an image of 'uncouth manner and aspect, stolid understanding, and snail-like movement.' He spoke with a

In Fordington Mead, by Henry Moule.
Photo: Dorset County Museum.

71

'chaotic corruption of regular language, that few persons ... consider it worth while to enquire what views, if any, of life, nature, or of society, are conveyed in these utterances.' 'He hangs his head and looks sheepish when spoken to, and thinks Lunnon (London) is a place paved with gold. Misery and fever lurk in his cottage...' and, 'He has few thoughts of joy, and little hope of rest...'.

For Hardy, however, this was an over-simplification. The language of the Dorsetshire labourers was, in fact, an agglomeration of English as taught at the National Schools which they attended, and the, 'unwritten, dying, Wessex English that they had learnt from their parents...'. Far from being uniformly joyless and dull; some were happy, many serene, and a few depressed. Some were clever, 'even to genius, some stupid, some wanton, some austere...'. Their political views were equally varied, and it was therefore a mistake to roll them all together into one. It was also a mistake to think that the 'grimiest families' were the poorest!

Years later, in March 1902, in a letter to author Henry Rider Haggard, Hardy developed his theme further. Up until about 1855 he said that the labourers' condition was one of great hardship. He had heard as a boy, of a 'sheep-keeping boy' (whose father's wages were a mere six shillings a week), who had died of hunger. At autopsy, the boy's stomach was found to contain nothing but undigested raw turnip. Since then, things had improved, noted Hardy. Now, it was not unusual to see a cottage with carpeting, with brass rods going up the staircase to keep the carpet in place. A piano might be found within, and a bicycle by the doorway. At night, a paraffin lamp was available.

Whilst these changes were welcome, others however, were not. The life-hold principle of tenancy applied, which had given the cottager security of tenure for three generations – a period of up to one hundred years – had now been replaced by weekly renewable agreements, leading to great insecurity. Now, if say an honest man's daughter were to have an illegitimate child, or if he or his wife took to drink, the family could be instantly evicted by the squire. 'The Damocles' sword of the poor,' said Hardy, 'is the fear of being turned out of their houses by the farmer or squire...'. For this reason, there was now a massive migration into the towns, which were not 'fraught with such trying consequences', as there were in the villages.

With the migration of the labourers, the village tradition began to decline 'into eternal oblivion'. With the absence of continuity of environment in their lives, so there was now no continuity of information. 'Names, stories, and relics' of a place were now 'speedily forgotten...'. [8.12] The effect on the labourers' children was equally deleterious. In 'shifting from school to school,' said Hardy, 'their education could not possibly progress with that regularity which is essential to their getting the best knowledge in the short time available to them.' [8.13]

9

Dorchester: Max Gate: *The Mayor of Casterbridge*: *The Woodlanders*: Italy

In June 1883, the Hardys moved to Dorchester, to lodgings in Shire Hall Lane. Two months later, they attended a church service at Winterborne Came, taken by clergyman and poet William Barnes. On this occasion, they were accompanied by Edmund Gosse, poet and man of letters, and a friend of Hardy for some years.

Unable to find a house in Dorchester, Hardy purchased a plot of land from the Duchy of Cornwall, situated a mile out of town to the east, on the road to Wareham. Here, he would build a house of his own, or rather, design it and get his brother Henry to construct it. The dwelling would be called 'Max Gate'; the name being derived from that of the inhabitant of a nearby toll gate-house, which was inhabited by a Mr Mack! During the digging out of the foundations some Romano-British graves, containing urns and skeletons, were discovered.

In June 1884, the day after Hardy's forty-fourth birthday, he went to a circus performance in nearby Fordington Field. June and July saw the couple again in London, meeting artists and writers including the painter Edward Burne-Jones. In July, Hardy visited the Dorchester Assizes, and in August a performance of Shakespeare's *Othello*, by strolling players at Dorchester. In August, Hardy and his brother visited the Channel Islands, taking the steamer from Weymouth. In December, Hardy attended the New Year's Eve bell ringing at Dorchester's Church of St Peter. He observed that the tenor bell was worn, and its clapper battered with its many strikes. [9.1]

Early in 1885, Hardy was invited to Eggesford, Devon, by his friend Lady Portsmouth, who with her husband encouraged the couple to move to Devonshire to be near them. Emma would have gone willingly Hardy records, as it was her native county. However, it was impracticable, as the Dorchester house was now nearing completion. [9.2]

On April 19, 1885, Hardy completed the writing of *The Mayor of Casterbridge*. It had taken at least a year, during which time he had been 'frequently interrupted...'. [9.3]

74

At Cokers Frome, by Henry Moule.
Photo: Dorset County Museum.

ᘒᘖ

The *Mayor of Casterbridge* was, in Hardy's own words, 'more particularly the study of one man's deeds and character...', and in this way it differs from his other novels. [9.4] This is Michael Henchard, a powerful, dominating man, who towers above the other characters in the novel, but nonetheless, is ultimately 'defeated by his own defects'. [9.5]

Henchard, a journeyman (hired workman) hay-trusser, arrives at 'Weydon Fair' in search of work. Here, while out of his mind through drink, Henchard puts his wife, Susan, up for auction. She is 'bought' by a wandering sailor called Newson, who departs with her, and her child by Henchard, Elizabeth Jane. Henchard now vows not to touch drink again for twenty years. He settles in 'Casterbridge' (Dorchester), where he prospers as a corn merchant, and ultimately becomes the town's mayor.

Years later, Susan reappears. She believes her husband to be drowned, and is in need of support for her daughter and herself. Henchard remarries Susan, believing Elizabeth Jane to be his child. In fact, she is actually Newson's, (Susan's first child, by Henchard and also named Elizabeth Jane, having died), a fact which Susan chooses to conceal from him. Henchard, however, on a previous business visit to Jersey, met one Lucetta Le Sueur, whom he intended to marry. He now writes to inform Lucetta that this is now impossible.

A young and able Scotsman, Donald Farfrae, arrives on the scene, and Henchard takes him on as his manager. Out of jealously at Farfrae's success, and his popularity in the town, Henchard then dismisses him.

Susan Henchard dies, but leaves a letter for her husband informing him of the truth about Elizabeth Jane. Henchard, however, has already told Elizabeth Jane that it is he who is her father!

Lucetta now arrives from Jersey, and takes Elizabeth Jane on as her companion; but instead of paying court to Henchard, she transfers her affections to Farfrae. Henchard, who is now even more jealous of his former manager, threatens to reveal the truth about Lucetta's former attachment to himself, and thereby blackmails Lucetta into promising that she will marry him.

Henchard comes to grief when, sitting as a magistrate, he is exposed in court as a one time wife-seller. His credibility is now lost, leaving Lucetta free to marry Farfrae; which she does. Now, the weather takes a hand.

In the words of Hardy himself, 'the home Corn Trade ... had an importance that can hardly be realised...'. [9.6] The entire population depended on the harvest, and 'After mid summer they (the farmers) watched the weather-cocks as men waiting in antechambers watch the lackey (obsequious manservant)'. [9.7] Henchard gambles unsuccessfully on the weather; and goes bankrupt. Farfrae, however, continues to prosper: the final indignity for Henchard being when Farfrae purchases Henchard's former house.

When a certain 'Royal Personage' passes through Casterbridge and Henchard makes a foolish exhibition of himself, Farfrae is forced to intervene. Henchard now challenges him to a fight to the death but relents, having got the Scotsman at his mercy. Henchard also relents about the love letters once sent to him by Lucetta (who is now pregnant by her husband). Instead of choosing to take revenge on her and Farfrae, Henchard agrees to return them to her. The plan misfires, and the shock of witnessing the townspeople parading an effigy of herself and Henchard through the streets, causes Lucetta to miscarry and die.

When Newson comes 'back from the dead', Henchard lies to him and tells him that Elizabeth Jane is also dead. Henchard disappears from the scene, revisits Casterbridge briefly for Elizabeth Jane's marriage to Farfrae, and then dies in an abandoned house in the presence of his former employee, Abel Whittle.

෬ඉ

Described as a 'smouldering, volcanic fellow', Henchard's pattern is 'to cheat himself of success, companionship, happiness, love...'. He is 'a confusing mixture of good and evil', but despite his 'negative qualities', he also possesses 'courage, generosity', and 'forthrightness'. [9.8] This is a man 'driven by inner destructive forces beyond his comprehension and control...'. [9.9] In short, Henchard illustrates the Darwinian 'Theory of Evolution' (which Hardy would have been familiar with), in that being unable to adapt, he is therefore unable to survive. His bitter experiences in life also bear out the notion held by Hardy's mother Jemima, that there is always a figure standing in our path to 'knock us back'.

As usual with Hardy *The Mayor of Casterbridge* is rooted in fact. There was a case in real life of a man selling his wife, and Prince Albert did actually visit Dorchester in July 1849. The anchor-character, rock solid and utterly dependable, who all too often appears in Hardy's novels, is here present in the character of Elizabeth Jane, who continues to demonstrate her concern for Henchard (despite all), right to the bitter end. If Hardy had ever had a daughter, how he would have loved her to be like Elizabeth Jane!

The Mayor of Casterbridge was published on May 10, 1886, by Smith, Elder.

෨෧

April 1885 found the Hardys again in London, viewing paintings at the Royal Academy, and attending a party given by Lady Carnarvon, wife of the 4th Earl, at which they met Conservative politician, Lord Salisbury.

When June came it was time to transfer the furniture from their Dorchester lodging house to their new house, Max Gate, described as an unpretending red brick structure of moderate size, standing on a 1½ acre plot of land. Hardy was soon to plant in excess of 2000 trees around the house; perhaps with a view to greater privacy and to protection from the gales. One of the first visitors to Max Gate was Scottish novelist, Robert Louis Stevenson, who was then living in Bournemouth in a house called 'Skerrymore'. In the drawing room of Max Gate, Hardy would write his next novel *The Woodlanders*.

A 'careful observer' described Hardy at this time as being 'below the middle-height' (he was actually 5foot 7inches tall), of 'slight build', with 'a pleasant, thoughtful face, exceptionally broad at the temples and fringed by a beard...'. He always wore a moustache, and his eyes were 'a clear, blue-grey'. [9.10]

William Barnes, formerly a teacher of Hardy, had retired from school-mastering in 1864, when he had been offered the living of Winterborne Came-cum-Whitcombe; the rectory of which stood not half a mile from Max Gate. In October, when Hardy visited him, Barnes told him how, when Prince Louis Napoleon was resident in England, he had visited the Damer family, with whom he was friendly, at Winterborne-Came House, near Dorchester. Hardy had already written one book set in Napoleonic times, *The Trumpet Major*. One day, his fascination with the period would lead him to write another, namely, *The Dynasts*. Hardy wrote *The Woodlanders* in the study above the drawing room at Max Gate. The plot caused him considerable anxiety, and he complained of a 'sick headache', and 'a fit of depression', in which he seemed to be 'enveloped in a leaden cloud'. [9.11] The end of the year 1885 made him 'sadder than many previous New Year's Eves have done'. He asked himself whether the building of Max Gate was 'a wise expenditure of energy', but hinted that there may have been darker forces at work, which had undermined his spirits.

∽∾

In London once again, in the spring and summer, he spent time in the British Museum's Reading Room, and attended the House of Commons where the Home Rule Bill for Ireland was being debated. In May he describes meeting a 'Hindu Buddhist', who spoke English fluently, was remarkably well educated, and was a 'coach' (tutor) of the Theosophical Society (which professes that a knowledge of God may be gained by intuitive insight into the nature of the divine). He went to his club, enjoyed observing trials at the Law Courts, and with Emma, attended dinners in private houses.

In October 1886, Hardy, in a letter to Edmund Gosse, describes how he has suffered previously at the hands of certain critics, in particular, the 'anonymous' critics who chose not to reveal their names. The 'crown of my bitterness', he says, 'has been my sense of unfairness in such impersonal means of attack...'. This misleads the public into thinking that there is 'an immense weight of opinion' behind the criticism, which one such as he, Hardy, can only oppose with his 'own little solitary personality...'. [9.12] Two months later, he makes use of this word again in a letter to journalist, William Rideing: 'My life when a boy was singu-

78

larly uneventful and solitary', he says. [9.13] That same month, Hardy's former schoolmaster and friend, the poet William Barnes, died at the age of eighty-five.

Hardy completed *The Woodlanders* on February 4, 1887, and recorded in his dairy that he felt relieved at having done so! [9.14]

☉

The novel *The Woodlanders*, involved in Hardy's own words 'the question of matrimonial divergence, the immortal puzzle ... how (are a couple) to find a basis for their sexual relation(ship)'. The problem arises when a person 'feels some second person to be better suited to his or her tastes than the one with whom he has contracted to live...'. This, on the one hand, may be viewed as the 'depravity' of an 'erratic heart'. But on the other hand, no thinking person concerned with the question of 'how to afford the greatest happiness to the units of human society during their brief transit through this sorry world...', would be content to let the matter rest here.

Implicit in this dilemma is the question of how marriage is viewed, whether as a divinely sanctioned 'covenant', 'What God hath joined together...', or as a simple secular 'contract' between two people? The very use of the word 'sexual', by Hardy in the Preface to *The Woodlanders*, daring by the standards of the time, reflects his own deep preoccupation with the subject.

☉

The Woodlanders begins with estate owner Mrs Charmond, demanding to have the locks of hair of Marty South, a poor girl who is assistant to Giles Winterborne, cider-maker and forester, and is the hero of the story. Straightaway, we have the upper class behaving as if they owned those whom they considered to be beneath them.

Timber merchant George Melbury has a daughter Grace, to whom he has given a good education. Whereas it was always assumed that one day Giles and Grace, to whom he was devoted, would marry, Grace's father intervenes and tells her that she is worthy of someone better, 'a man who can take you up in society, out into the world'.

An incident which reveals Hardy's impish sense of humour occurs

79

when Giles invites the Melburys to a 'gathering', at which Grace discovers a slug in her 'leaves of winter-green'. When the guests have departed, Giles' servant reassures his master that the slug was well boiled. 'I warrant him well boiled. God forbid that a live slug should seed on any plate of victuals that's served by Robert Creedle...'! [9.15]

Edred Fitzpiers arrives on the scene to take up the position of local doctor. When Giles loses some properties which he owns, and becomes less eligible on this account, Melbury points his daughter in the direction of Dr Fitzpiers.

Mrs Charmond's carriage, and Giles' waggon meet head to head in the lane. Giles is unable to reverse, and Mrs Charmond, who sees this as insubordination, announces that she is to demolish his cottage for a road-widening scheme, yet another example in Hardy's eyes, of the callousness of the upper classes.

Grace and Fitzpiers duly marry, but when Fitzpiers tells Grace that they can now no longer consort socially with such lowly people as her brothers, Grace tells her father that she feels the doctor is ashamed 'of us, of me'. When Grace discovers that Fitzpiers is a liar, and that he has been philandering with Mrs Charmond, she and her father realise that the marriage was a great mistake.

George Melbury believes that the law will enable his daughter to divorce Fitzpiers, but in this he is mistaken; because 'your husband has not been cruel enough'. 'The law will leave you as Mrs Fitzpiers 'till the end of the chapter', he says. Again, Hardy is revealing his distaste for legal statutes which condemn men and women to lives of misery.

Fitzpiers accompanies Mrs Charmond to the continent. When he returns looking for Grace, she leaves home and flees to Giles' hut. Giles, mindful of her reputation as a married woman, spends several nights sleeping outdoors in the open. He succumbs to a sickness and dies; to be mourned by Grace, and also by Marty South, who also loved him. At Grace and Fitzpiers' final meeting, the doctor, now contrite, asks Grace what she feels for him. 'Nothing', is the answer.

ৎ৯

Why did Hardy choose to focus on this particular aspect of life at this particular time? Did it preoccupy his mind because he himself was unhappy in his own relationship? A forthcoming visit to the continent by himself and Emma, would shortly shed more light on this question.

⟨∽⟩

The Woodlanders contains a detailed description of man traps, spring-loaded devices made of iron (and designed with teeth to lacerate the flesh, and crush the bones) which were placed on paths to catch poachers. Although the use of such devices had largely died out by the mid-nineteenth century, Hardy would have seen them as yet another example of oppression, not to say barbaric brutality, by those who should have known better.

⟨∽⟩

On March 14, 1887, Hardy and Emma left Dorchester for London, en route to Italy. Here, they visited the cathedrals of Pisa and Milan; the Colosseum, and the graves of the poets Shelley and Keats at Rome; all indicative of Hardy's reverence for architecture and poetry. Venice, however, was the city which he appeared to enjoy the most. In Florence they visited the tomb of Elizabeth Browning, poet and wife of Robert, who had died in 1861; and also Lucy Baxter, daughter of Hardy's former mentor, the Dorset poet William Barnes, who had settled there after her marriage.

Emma, in her diaries, revealed some of the tensions that existed between the two of them at this time. 'Tom very vexed'; 'Tom has taken another little stroll by himself'; 'Tom ... had an altercation (with the father of a family) about seats'; this was on the train journey from Italy to Paris, where Emma admitted to siding with the father of the family in question, against her husband. These remarks point to the fact that their marriage was not in the healthy and robust state which might have been expected.

The words 'Little shoe-black [presumably a refererence to a child whose job it was to polish the shoes of visitors] persistent at Forum [in Rome] ... broke my umbrella beating him off', may be construed as the sign of a certain contempt on Emma's part for the underprivileged.

10

Inner Thoughts: *Wessex Tales*: *A Group of Noble Dames*: *Tess of the D'Urbervilles*

In London again in the spring of 1887, Hardy and Emma trod the well-known path to society gatherings, and met the poet Robert Browning, with whom they discussed their recent holiday in Italy. June 28 was the occasion of Queen Victoria's Jubilee, and they went to see the procession, which included vast numbers of royalty.

In August 1887, in a letter to his friend, the poet and critic Edmund Gosse, Hardy told of the weeks and months of 'despondency' which he had experienced 'in byegone years', the most recent bout being 'several years ago' (and presumably including the time of his married life with Emma). This, he attributed to his 'stomach' and eating habits, but conceded that this may not always have been the cause. In the autumn, Hardy was toying with ideas for plots for his forthcoming novel *The Dynasts*. Meanwhile, his reading of the poets and the classics continued unabated.

In the spring of 1888, they spent time in London before travelling again to Paris, to the Salon, to the races at Longchamps, and to an exhibition of drawings and paintings by French writer Victor Hugo. [10.1] On their return, Hardy called upon Lady Portsmouth, and (always one with an eye for a pretty face or figure) remarked upon how well her ladyship's 'black, brocaded silk' fitted her!

&

On May 4, Hardy's *Wessex Tales*, a collection of short stories, was published by Macmillan. They included, 'The Three Strangers', in which the hangman meets his victim-to-be, an escaped convict, in a shepherd's cottage; 'The Withered Arm', where a woman invokes magic to cure a malady; and 'A Tradition of Eighteen Hundred and Four', where Napoleon (with whom Hardy is always fascinated), is engaged in a reconnaissance of the Wessex countryside! In 'The Distracted Preacher', Hardy makes use of anecdotes told to him by his grandfather

Thomas I, in painting a picture of smuggling on the 'Wessex' coast!

In mid-July, they returned to Dorchester, where Hardy recorded interesting stories which he had heard for possible inclusion in future novels. Examples were the man who took 'casts of the heads of executed convicts'; and the young lady who got married wearing 'a dainty pair of shoes' previously thrown at her by another man whose love she had spurned; he was a shoemaker, and had made them for her as a present.

In London in 1889, Hardy was fascinated by the use of light by Turner in his paintings at an exhibition at the Royal Academy. He also compared the techniques of Botticelli and Rubens in their depiction of the 'flesh', vis-a-vis the 'soul'; the fact that both these men were portrayers of the female form par excellence, would not have been wasted on him! As always, the couple attended church services, concerts, plays, and of course, society events!

In April, in a letter to poet and essayist, John Addington Symonds, Hardy asks 'whether we ought to write sad stories, considering how much sadness there is in the world already?' However, he concludes that the justification for doing so is that, 'the first step towards cure of, or even relief from, and disease (is)... to understand it'. This may then provide an escape from the worst forms of it (i.e. sadness), in real life. [10.2]

&

At the end of July 1889, the Hardys returned to Max Gate where Hardy settled into the daily routine of writing what would be his next novel *Tess of the D'Urbervilles*. This was not, however, to be a straightforward project. The first two magazines to whom he sent it rejected the manuscript on the grounds that it was 'improper', and it was only after Hardy had laboriously edited it, by removing some, or all of various chapters, that it was finally accepted by the editor of the weekly newspaper, the *Graphic*.

Hardy, despite the labour of writing, still found the time and energy to record his thoughts and feelings on those subjects which he found intriguing. For example, religion; he had been searching for God for fifty years he confessed, 'and I think that if he had existed I should have discovered him'. [10.3] He also found time to write to Hugh Thackeray Turner, secretary to the Society for the Protection of Ancient Buildings. Hardy objected to the proposed demolition of the church in the village of Stratton, near Dorchester, when in his view, some 'judicious repair' was all that was necessary. [10.4]

At Easter 1890, Hardy visited the grave of William Barnes at Winterborne-Came. In May, when he and Emma were again in London, Hardy sent the manuscript of *A Group of Noble Dames* to the *Graphic*, who agreed to serialise it. This was a collection of short stories, the background for which Hardy drew heavily on *The History and Antiquities of the County of Dorset*, by the Reverend John Hutchins (first published in 1774). In the words of one critic, it was a 'pageant of disastrous marriages, confessed and unconfessed adulteries, complicated illegitimacies, sudden deaths, suspected crimes', and 'bizarre cruelties ... among the Wessex gentry of some generations back...'.[10.5] Hardy obtained his information for this from 'the lips of aged people in a remote part of the country where traditions of the local families linger on, and are remembered by the yeomen and peasantry long after they are forgotten by the families concerned'. [10.6] A year later *A Group of Noble Dames* was published in book form by Osgood, McIlvaine & Co. of London.

At the end of June, Hardy said he was 'getting tired of investigating life at music halls and police courts', which appears to have been his principal preoccupation during that season in London. Attendance at the latter would probably have provided material for his stories, and also satisfied his somewhat morbid curiosity, whereas the beautiful actresses and dancers with their 'lustrous eyes and pearly countenances' which he would have seen at the former, would have given him light relief and titillation.

When Emma's father John Gifford died, she left the capital to attend his funeral in Devon. Hardy did not accompany her. Thereafter Hardy arranged annuities for Emma's niece Lilian, and her nephew Gordon, who spent long periods with him and Florence at Max Gate. In fact it was with Hardy's encouragment that Gordon became an architect. That August, Hardy and his brother Henry went together on a visit to Paris.

ᕐᕐ

It may have afforded Hardy some amusement to consider that he, an outspoken critic (through his writings) of the upper classes was now coming into contact more and more, not only with London society, but also with the gentry of Dorset. He met people such as Mrs Brinsley Sheridan (a descendant of Irish dramatist Richard Brinsley Sheridan) of Frampton Court, Frampton, near Dorchester whose ball he attended in the January of 1891. For this, Emma arrived on horseback; horse riding being a favourite pastime of hers. Sadly she would never ride again.

In the Spring of 1891, Hardy was elected to the Athenaeum (London literary club). However, despite his literary success, he was still unable to afford a second home in London, and therefore he and Emma were obliged to find rented accommodation for their annual spring sojourns in the capital. It was from the balcony of the Athenaeum that Hardy saw the German Emperor William II pass by. At a luncheon at Mary Jeune's (Lady St Helier, wife of Francis, a distinguished judge) in July, he mentions sitting between 'a pair of beauties' (women), one who had violet eyes and was 'seductive', and the other who was 'more vivacious'. [10.7]

In September, Hardy and Emma visited Scotland and many of the places depicted by Sir Walter Scott in his novels. In November, Hardy gave his opinion on whether eminent men of letters should be awarded national recognition. The problem as he saw it, was that while 'the highest flights of the pen (by an author) are mostly the excursions and revelations of souls unreconciled to life...', the 'natural tendency of a government' was to encourage acquiescence in life as it is.' [10.8] When Emma's mother died, it is not known if Emma attended the funeral.

෨෧

Despite mixing in high society, Hardy remained true to himself and his beliefs, for he was now engaged in writing a very human story entitled *Tess of the D'Urbervilles*. Hardy appeared to derive inspiration from beginning a new book in a different location, and to this end he moved out of his old study and into a new one situated at the rear of Max Gate, with a window facing west.

It begins with Parson Tringham, antiquary, addressing Jack Durbeyfield, a 'haggler' (itinerant dealer) as 'Sir John', and informing him that he was descended from the 'ancient and knightly family of the D'Urbervilles'. [10.9] Hardy describes Jack as a 'slack-twisted fellow', whose times (of work) could not be relied on to coincide with the hours of requirement (of his employer)...' – Hardy's wit! [10.10]

When John's wife informs him that a great lady by the name of D'Urberville is living at nearby Trantridge (Pentridge, near Cranborne), it is decided that their daughter Tess, should pay them a visit with the purpose of claiming kinship to them.

In the course of Tess's visit she meets the young man of the house, Alec, who confesses that his family are not genuine 'D'Urbervilles', but bought the title of this 'old, extinguished family'. The outcome is that Alec's mother offers Tess a job managing her poultry farm. The old lady is deeply attached to her fowls and although she is blind, is able to recognise each one of them individually by its comb, beak and claws.

On hearing from Tess that her family's horse has died, Alec generously provides them with another. He then seduces her, but after being mistress to him for a period of four months, Tess returns home where she has his baby. However, when the vicar arrives to baptise the infant, Tess's father refuses to allow him to do so; his family having suffered such disgrace. When the child dies, Tess informs the vicar that she herself has previously baptised it. Nevertheless, the vicar refuses to allow a Christian burial.

Tess then finds employment with farmer Crick, described as a 'kindly man who has his own pew in church...'. Amongst his employees is one Angel Clare (Hardy having obtained the name 'Angel' from a memorial plaque in Stinsford church), a parson's son who wishes to become a farmer. When the butter refuses to set, this is taken to mean that someone is in love – Hardy's appreciation of folklore. This is true, the loving couple being Angel and Tess. Angel proposes to Tess, she accepts, and they marry.

When Angel confesses to having had a brief relationship with an older woman, Tess forgives him. However when, despite her mother warning her against it, Tess confesses to her relationship with Alec, resulting in the birth of the child, now deceased, Angel takes this as proof that she is the 'last in the line of degenerate aristocrats', and departs for Brazil. Tess returns home. She now has to endure jeering, and being referred to as a 'trollope'. [10,11]

Tess now endures great hardship working in the fields uprooting turnips and feeding wheat into the threshing machine, which works remorselessly from dawn to dusk. Meanwhile, she resists the overtures of Alec, who tells her that had he known her circumstances, he would have done his duty by the child. Aware that Tess's father is ill and the

Woolbridge Manor and Chapel where Tess and Angel spent their honeymoon, by Henry Moule. Photo: Dorset County Museum.

family liable to be evicted, Alec offers his help, but is again rejected. To be fair to Alec, he does offer to marry Tess, but she declines because she does not love him. Sure enough, Jack Durbeyfield dies and the family is rendered homeless.

Angel returns home to find letters of desperation from Tess, which have not been forwarded. He goes looking for her, and eventually finds her in Sandbourne. He asks her forgiveness, she tells him it is too late. She is now living with Alec who has been good to her family, and has won her back to him. A distraught Angel catches the train home, only to have Tess jump into the carriage and join him. She has murdered Alec!

The couple flee, Angel being determined to save her. However, finally at the 'pagan temple' of Stonehenge, she is captured.

ᏩᏩ

In *Tess of the D'Urbervilles*, Hardy's heroine Tess, who demonstrates her human frailty by her brief dalliance with Alec, is set on a course of destruction, culminating with her being hanged for murder at 'Wintonchester' (Winchester). Her second 'mistake' was of being honest. She wanted to have no secrets from Angel, he must know the truth.

Tess showed immense qualities of endurance in resisting Alec, who provided the easy way out but whom she did not love, and remaining true to Angel, even though he had forsaken her. The forces which crushed Tess were enshrined by an establishment which condemned adultery, and the having of illegitimate children, 'bastardy'. For this, Tess was punished by being jeered at, and denied a Christian burial for her child. However, the impact of this on her life would not have been so catastrophic had it not been for Angel's intolerance and bigotry in assessing Tess's 'lapse' to be of greater significance than his own. In short, Tess was literally hounded to her death by the combined harshness of the establishment and of those around her.

ᘒ

The theme of a person such as Tess being descended from a distinguished family finds echoes in Hardy's own background. Just as the knowledge of it was a millstone for the Durbeyfields, who made desperate but futile efforts to live up to the 'knightliness' of their ancestry, so it may have been for Hardy; after all, for him the theme is seldom far away. It is difficult therefore to believe that what Hardy perceived as his lack of 'pedigree', as it were, was not a matter of deep resentment to him.

Undoubtedly, Tess provided Hardy with a vehicle for yet another outburst against oppression. Is it possible, however, that he also derived a certain satisfaction from her discomfiture? Tess carried self reproach almost to the point of masochism when, having struck Alec on the mouth, she invites him to punish her. 'Whip me, crush me...', she cries, 'I shall not cry out. Once victim, always victim, that's the law.'. [10.12] In having Tess hanged at the end, Hardy was certainly reliving the hanging of Elizabeth Brown at Dorchester, which he had witnessed personally in the year 1856 when he was aged fifteen.

ᘒ

Tess of the D'Urbervilles was published in late November, 1891, by Osgood, McIlvaine. The novel became a talking point throughout the land, and was quickly translated into several languages, including Russian. Despite this, many libraries refused to stock it. Its review in *The Quarterly* was to offend Hardy deeply. The article, he said, was smart and amusing, but at the expense of truth and sincerity. 'If this sort of thing (criticism) continues,' he said, then there would be 'no more novel writing for me.' [10.13]

ᏬᎥ

On July 20, 1892, Hardy's father died. Like Horatio in Shakespeare's *Hamlet*, he had in his lifetime taken suffering and fortune 'with equal thanks'. His last request had been for a drink of water from the well, which led him, when he had tasted it, to say, 'Now I know I am at home.' He was buried in Stinsford churchyard, and Hardy himself made the design for his father's tombstone. From then on, the family business was carried on by Hardy's brother Henry. That October also saw the death of Tennyson, whose funeral in Westminster Abbey Hardy attended.

ᏬᎥ

The following May, 1893, Hardy and Emma visited Ireland, where in Dublin they met Florence Henniker (sister of Lord Houghton, the Lord Lieutenant, and wife of Arthur Henniker-Major, an army officer) with whom Hardy was to strike up a long friendship and correspondence. They were present in the city for Queen Victoria's Birthday Review, held on the 24th of that month.

June found Hardy in Oxford, at a time when the Commemoration proceedings were taking place (to honour the University's founders and benefactors); the purpose of the visit being to gather material for his next novel. The previous year, Hardy had visited the village of Great Fawley in Berkshire, from where his maternal grandmother, Mary Head, who had experienced a miserable life as an orphan, had originated. The hero of his next novel, Jude Fawley, would derive his name from this village: the novel would be entitled, *Jude the Obscure*.

In August, Hardy and Emma spent some time in Wales. In November, he wrote two poems, and on Christmas Eve at Max Gate, they received the carol singers who, with their lanterns, stood under the trees and sang to the accompaniment of a harmonium.

11

Jude the Obscure

In February 1894, Hardy's remaining short stories were published by Osgood, McIlvaine, under the title *Life's Little Ironies*. The Hardys again rented accommodation in London, taking their servants with them, and spending the spring in their customary way viz. attending dinners, plays, and the theatre.

That April, Hardy wrote to his friend Edward Clodd to say that years ago, an old woman had confirmed his assertion that every superstition, custom, etcetera, described in his novels were based 'on true records of the same...' and were not inventions of his own. [11.1]

In September, 1895, Hardy in a letter advised Florence Henniker to read systematically. 'Stick to a few books and read these over and over again,' he said, and only now and then introduce, 'some really valuable new book as a sauce (i.e. to give piquancy)...'. [11.2]

Hardy, at Max Gate, was obliged to alter *Jude the Obscure* to suit *Harper's Magazine*, in which it was serialised, beginning in the November. He then had to restore it to its original state. Despite this exhausting process, the work was published a year later, in November 1895, again by Osgood, McIlvaine. The novel, said Hardy, who was now aged fifty-five, was intended for men and women of 'full (adult) age'. It attempted to deal with 'the fret and fever, derision and disaster, that may press in the wake of the strongest passion known to humanity...'; in other words, the passion evoked by physical attraction. This, he said, 'was a deadly war waged between flesh and spirit...'. [11.3] However, further examination reveals that this is no abstract debate by Hardy on the subject of sexual compatibility. Instead, there is every reason to believe that he was speaking from bitter personal experience! In fact, *Jude the Obscure* tells us more about this aspect of Hardy than any of his other published writings.

෧෨

Schoolmaster Mr Phillotson's advice to his pupil Jude, hero of the story, is 'be kind to animals and birds, and read all you can.' [11.4] Miss Fawley was Jude's great-aunt, and her advice to him was to get Phillotson 'to take 'ee

Thomas Hardy in the 1890s.
Photo: Dorset County Museum.

(Jude) to Christminster (Oxford) wi' un (him), and make a scholar of 'ee'. She also cautioned Jude against marriage. '... don't you ever marry', she said. 'Tisn't for the Fawleys to take that step any more.' [11.5]

Straightaway, therefore, Hardy has introduced several concepts which are meaningful to him. One is a concern for animals, such as a pig which has to be slaughtered. In Jude's remarks about a creature which he loves and mourns after its death, Hardy manages to convey both a sense of tragedy, combined with native humour and wit. But of Hardy's real feelings there is no doubt. He had introduced this episode into the novel 'to serve a humane end', by 'showing people the cruelty that goes on unheeded under the barbarous regime we call civilisation.' [11.6] This, said Hardy, had been a great grief to him for years. [11.7] Another is the value of a sound education, Christminster becoming in Jude's mind, a romanticised place of scholars who work in the rarified atmosphere of high academia. And a third is the view that some people are congenitally unsuited for marriage.

Despite the fact that Jude's great-aunt continually reiterates the idea that the Fawleys were not made for wedlock, Jude is tricked into marriage to Arabella Donn, daughter of a pig breeder.

Jude longs to use his talents, and to have them recognised. His cousin Sue Bridehead, on the other hand, dreams of being unconventional; a free spirit. Unlike Jude, Sue sees the Saints as the stuff of legend rather than of reality [11.8] and Christminster as a place where intellect is pushing one way and religion the other 'like two rams butting each other'. 'The mediaevalism of Christminster must be sloughed off,' she declares, 'or Christminster itself will have to go.' [11.9] This statement reflects Hardy's own inner struggle to reconcile the intellect with the turgid dogma of Christianity.

Jude's ambition is to go to Christminster, where they raise parsons 'like radishes in a bed' (Hardy's wonderful imagery); [11.10] but this is blocked by the university authorities. He is a stonemason, therefore he cannot be a scholar, not officially, at any rate. In this, Hardy was not writing from personal experience (he appears not to have made any serious attempt to enter university, despite the encouragement of Horace Moule), but making the general point that university was a 'closed shop', so to speak, and 'open' only to the privileged few.

Although the church blesses his union to Arabella, Jude sees it as a marriage in name only. Would it not be better, therefore, if marriage was a secular contract between two people, rather than a religious one? Arabella goes to Australia and, for the time being, that is the last he hears of her. Now, he falls in love with Sue, but there are problems here also. She has a dread, she declares, 'lest an iron contract should extinguish your tenderness for me, and mine for you.' She and Jude should live as lovers. The moment one is 'contracted to cherish ... under a Government stamp... Ugh, how horrible and sordid.' [11.11] Jude agrees that marriage may mean buying a month of pleasure followed by a lifetime of discomfort. However, he is grieved that Sue is elusive, and has never once made the honest declaration that she loves him. When it comes to where to get married, Jude and Sue are torn between the vulgarity of the Registrar's Office and the 'awful solemnity' of the church. 'Let us go home,' says Sue, 'without killing our dream.' [11.12]

Then comes an event which brings the secular versus religious conflict into sharp relief. Jude is employed by the church to inscribe a stone tablet with words from the Ten Commandments which include, 'Thou shalt not commit adultery'; but when he is recognised as one who is doing this very thing, he is told that his services are no longer required. Arabella informs Jude that, unbeknown to him, he has a son 'little Jude'. She has returned from Australia and wishes Jude to give him a home, which he and Sue agree to. However, the fact that Jude and Sue are unmarried leads the family being turned out of the lodgings which they occupy in Christminster.

When Commemoration day (which Hardy calls, 'Remembrance day') dawns, and the university remembers its former founders and benefactors, Jude sees it rather as 'humiliation day', for despite all his knowledge, gained from long years of study, he is still an outsider. He has now become disillusioned.

When their children, now three in number, including little Jude, commit suicide, Sue regards it as a judgment from God. Still, Jude longs for Sue's affection. It is his great regret that she has never really loved him, as he loves her.

෪ඞ

There was a longstanding belief that the Hardys were descended from a family, once great but now in decline, and it is possible that Hardy himself had an inferiority complex on this account. But might he also

93

have felt the same about Emma's family, her father a solicitor, having failed so miserably in his chosen profession?

A writer is at his most profound when he is discussing a subject of which he has personal experience, and no one can say that *Jude the Obscure* is not a profound book. Jude longs for emotional and physical love and warmth, but in Sue he fails to find it. Could the same be true of Hardy in relation to Emma? Hardy's use of the phrase, the 'tragedy of unfulfilled aims' in the Preface, provides a strong hint that this indeed may have been the case. There is also a curious poem written by Hardy in Bournemouth in 1875 (the year following his marriage to Emma), which ends: 'Wasted were two souls in their prime,/ And great was the waste that July time/ When the rain came down.'

Another poem entitled 'To a Sea Cliff', written at Durlston Head near Swanage, ends in a similar curious way: 'He slid apart/ Who had thought her heart/ His own, and not aboard/ A bark, sea-bound..../ That night they found/ Between them lay a sword.' (Hardy is known to have been in Swanage in 1875, so this poem was probably written in this year also.)

Could this powerful image of a 'sword' which Hardy refers to, be the barrier which Emma put up to his physical advances? And did this barrier remain through the years, until finally Hardy could contain himself no longer and vented all his frustrations, bitterness and anguish through the voice of the equally agonised Jude?

In his characters, plots and locations, Hardy was the master of disguise; but for once he had been found out! The relationship between Jude and Sue was in many ways similar to his own relationship with Emma. For her part, Emma, having realised that this was the case by identifying certain aspects of the story with her own life, felt that she had come out of it badly and been portrayed in a poor light. She had, as it were, read between the lines and in consequence, after the publication of *Jude the Obscure*, the rift between the two of them grew wider than ever.

For years Hardy had been searching without success for God. He had entered into his marriage to Emma with high hopes and expectations and had vowed in church to love, comfort, honour, and keep her, 'so long as ye both shall live'. Within a short time, however, he realised that the marriage lacked the one fundamental thing that he craved, sexual fulfilment, the ultimate manifestation of his love for Emma, and hers for him.

Now he felt bitter, particularly about the Christian church in which he had all but lost faith, and which had obliged him to make these vows on his wedding day. How much more preferable a secular contract, which by its nature was reversible, would have been to the Christian-sponsored life sentence of unrequited love which was now his lot. Hardy, like many of the characters in his novels, had become a victim. He had sublimated his own will to the Christian ethos with which he had been brought up, and to the strict social mores of the times. His philosophy and Sue's represented the opposite ends of the spectrum; two protagonists which were fighting a terrible battle of attrition within his soul. The effort of controlling his emotions and (thwarted) desires for all those long years must truly have been a superhuman one.

Just before Jude died, he uttered these words from the Bible's Book of Job: 'Let the day perish wherein I was born, and the night in which it was said, There is a man conceived.' 'Let that day be darkness; let not God regard it from above, neither let the light shine upon it. Lo, let that night be solitary, let no joyful voice come therein.' And it continues, 'Why died I not from the womb? Why did I not give up the ghost when I came out of the belly? ... For now I should have lain still and been quiet. I should have slept: then had I been at rest!' Was this how Hardy himself felt? Was it a source of regret to him that, at his birth, the vigilant nurse noticed that he was still alive when he was thought to be dead, and thereby saved his life? If so, it is impossible to read these lines without feeling an unutterable sadness for him.

Jude the Obscure also sheds light on a possible reason why Hardy did not opt to become a clergyman. The reason he gave was that this would have meant for him a prolonged period of study, but surely, for a man like Hardy, this would have presented no problem? No, it seems that there may have been a more fundamental reason. When Jude kisses Sue, and experiences all the pleasure of that moment of intimacy, he realises how 'glaringly inconsistent' it would be for him to pursue 'the idea of becoming ... a servant of religion', when that religion (in this case Christianity), regarded sexual love 'at its best as a frailty, and at its worst a damnation.' [11.13] In making this decision, Hardy was following Polonius' advice to his son Laertes, in Shakespeare's *Hamlet*, when he advised him 'To thine own self be true...'

☙

The 'earthquake' which followed the publication of *Jude the Obscure* was

95

of even greater magnitude than that which had followed *Tess of the D'Urbervilles*. This led Hardy to explain in a letter to 'a close friend', more about the character of Jude. [11.14] Sue and Jude occupied separate (bed) rooms, said Hardy, except towards the end. One of Sue's reasons for fearing the marriage ceremony was that she feared it would be 'breaking faith with Jude to withhold herself (presumably from sexual intercourse) at pleasure, or altogether, after it (the marriage)'. This had 'tended to keep his (Jude's) passions as hot at the end as at the beginning, and helps break his heart. He has never really possessed her as freely as he desired.' Surely, this is an exact statement by Hardy of his own position, vis-a-vis Emma!

In January 1896, Hardy complained that *Jude the Obscure* had been misinterpreted. The theme of 'the doom of hereditary temperament and unsuitable mating in marriage', had been taken as an attack on that institution in general. He also denied that the book was in any way immoral. [11.15] The following month he complained of 'fearful depression', and a 'slight headache...'. [11.16]

A section of the press chose to ignore Hardy and his works following the publication of *Jude the Obscure*, which it greeted with outrage and disgust. The Bishop of Wakefield announced that he had thrown the novel into the fire! Hardy later remarked dryly that, 'theology and burning' had been associated for many centuries, and supposed that they would continue to be allies to the end. [11.17]

Nevertheless, the London season of 1896 carried on regardless, and Hardy and Emma continued their acquaintance with such people as Susan, Countess of Malmesbury (a writer), the Duchess of Montrose, Theresa, Lady Londonderry, and the author Henry James. That August the couple visited Stratford-on-Avon, where they visited places associated with William Shakespeare. September saw them in France and in Belgium where Emma, who had by now given up horse riding, purchased a bicycle which she imported into England. Hardy revisited the site of the Battle of Waterloo; another novel based on the epic struggle between Emperor Napoleon and the Duke of Wellington was shortly to materialise. In June, Hardy wrote from London to his sister Katharine, offering to obtain for her 'pianoforte pieces', or 'dance music' from the music publisher Chappell. [11.18]

In October 1896, Hardy complained that when he stated in 'a passionate poem', that the 'Supreme Mover... (i.e. God) must be either limited in power, unknowing, or cruel...', then this went against the 'inert, crystallised opinion' of 'the vast body of men', who then assailed him for being a 'clamorous atheist'; whereas in fact he was a 'harmless agnostic'.

⊙⊙

In a postscript to *Jude the Obscure*, written some years later, Hardy made further comments on the novel and on its reception by the public and the critics; an experience which, he declared, completely cured him of further interest in novel writing. The marriage laws, he said, were 'used in great part as the tragic machinery of the tale'. His opinion, which had not changed over the years, was that 'a marriage should be dissolvable as soon as it becomes a cruelty to either of the parties', it then having become 'essentially and morally no marriage'. Hardy, for once had expressed a personal opinion in the most forthright terms; his enlightened views on the state of matrimony, formed no doubt from the experience of the wretched state of his own union, were far in advance of their time.

12

The Well-Beloved: Wessex Poems

Although The Well-Beloved (originally entitled The Pursuit of the Well-Beloved) was published (by Osgood, McIlvaine) in March 1897, the bulk of it was written before the publication of Jude the Obscure. This is a novel which stretches both imagination and credulity, but is successful in that it introduces the reader to a concept which he or she may be subconsciously aware of, but may not have hitherto heard articulated. That is, the idea that a person may fall in love, and continue to do so throughout his or her life, not with a particular being, but with a notion of perfect beauty, what Hardy called 'The Well-Beloved', which may temporarily reside in an actual person, but is fleeting and soon transmigrates to inhabit somebody else!

☙

The story is set on the 'Isle of Slingers' (Portland Island, in Dorset), and its hero is the twenty-year-old Jocelyn Pierston, who is a sculptress (many of Hardy's characters are either architects or sculptors). Pierston's 'Well-Beloved' 'was perhaps of no tangible substance', but rather 'a spirit, a dream, a frenzy, a conception, an aroma, an epitomised sex, a light of the eye, a parting of the lips.' 'He (Pierston) loved the masquerading creature wherever he found her, whether with blue eyes, black, or brown.' [12.1]

For Pierston, the 'Well-Beloved' is first 'embodied' in Avice Caro, a boyhood sweetheart. The couple become engaged, but by this time the embodiment had transferred itself to Marcia Bencomb, a local beauty. However, before he can propose to her, she leaves him and he finds a new incarnation of the 'Well-Beloved' in a high society widow Nichola Pine-Avon. Twenty years later, Avice dies. Pierston returns to the island for her funeral and meets her daughter, also called Avice. Pierston realises that embodiment has transferred itself to Avice II, however, she too is susceptible to 'Well-Beloveds'; she has already had no less than fifteen male embodiments herself, but even worse for Pierston, it transpires that she is already married. Another twenty years pass, and

Pierston duly falls in love with Avice II's daughter, Avice III! She, however, on learning of his former attachments not only to her mother, but also to her grandmother, leaves him for a younger man, who is the son of Pierston's former 'Well-Beloved', Marcia. Pierston admits that whenever he 'grapples with the reality of the 'Well-Beloved', 'she's no longer in it', so he is unable to 'stick to one incarnation' even if he wishes to. [12.2] Pierston finally marries Marcia, who by this time is an invalid.

⚭

Regarding the theme of *The Well-Beloved* it was Hardy's view that 'all men are pursuing a shadow, the Unattainable...'. This, he hoped, might 'redeem the tragi-comedy from the charge of frivolity'. In other words, Hardy did not wish to seem irresponsible by condoning flirtation and infidelity. Psychologists of today recognise that every person's psyche contains both male and female elements, described as the 'animus' and the 'anima' respectively. This begs the question, had Pierston therefore fallen in love with the female part of his own psyche, his 'anima'?

⚭

What was in Hardy's mind when he wrote this particular novel, whose theme was the migratory passion of a man, although as is evident, this characteristic could apply equally to a woman? His own marriage was causing him much grief evidently, on account of the absence of physical warmth and intimacy. On the other hand, when he was in London, he was constantly surrounded by beautiful women, whether at dinner parties, the theatre or music halls. What could be more natural, therefore, than for him to look longingly at such women, and think to himself, if only...? Also, he may have thought wistfully of all the attractive young ladies he had known before meeting Emma, and again thought, if only....

The most plausible explanation appears to be that for Hardy, the 'Well-Beloved' no longer resided in his wife Emma. Instead, it had migrated, and perhaps continued to do so, to other women; two of the main contenders for the new embodiment being Florence Henniker, wife of the army officer, and the beautiful Lady Agnes Grove, author and daughter of General and the Honourable Mrs Pitt-Rivers.

Was Hardy ever unfaithful to Emma? It is unlikely that anyone will ever know for sure, but his biographer Evelyn Hardy, is adamant that he was not. 'Hardy ... never broke away from the moral code,' she writes, 'which many of his protagonists had transgressed.' [12.3] Nevertheless, the effort of controlling his emotions and (thwarted) desires was a truly superhuman one! Stoical is perhaps the word that describes him best. He had made his vows, and he would stick to them come what may, and whatever the cost to his own well-being.

⁂

In January 1897, Hardy wrote to Edward Clodd in scathing terms of how 'theology' had been responsible for the arrest of 'light and reason' for 1600 years. So-called 'Christianity', he said, with its 'terrible, dogmatic ecclesiasticism', had 'hardly anything in common' with the real teachings of Christ. [12.4] That same month, he wrote to Florence Henniker expressing his admiration for the poet Shelley. Of all the men whom he (Hardy) would like to meet 'in the Elysian field', he said, he would choose Shelley, not only for his 'unearthly, weird, wild appearance and genius', but for his 'Genuineness, earnestness, and enthusiasms on behalf of the oppressed'. Truly, Hardy believed himself to be a kindred spirit of that great poet!

⁂

In 1897, the Hardys departed from their usual routine of renting accommodation in London, and instead opted to stay at Basingstoke, fifty or so miles away, and commute to the capital every few days.

In June, the occasion of Queen Victoria's Diamond Jubilee, they travelled to Switzerland to escape the crowds. On their return, they visited Wells and its cathedral, the ancient ruins of Stonehenge, and Salisbury where they attended a service in the cathedral.

Hardy's prodigious efforts on the literary front did not prevent him from taking a keen interest in local architectural affairs. In September he was advising architect Hugh Thackeray Turner on necessary repairs and maintenance to the tower of East Lulworth church, and in October advised him about the re-thatching and re-flooring of the White Horse Inn at Maiden Newton. [12.5] As he visited the latter site on a bicycle, and had therefore incurred no expenses, he told Turner that no repayment was necessary. The writer, Rudyard Kipling, joined Hardy for some of his cycling excursions, the latter having purchased a new bicycle, a Rover Cob. [12.6]

The following year, 1898, saw Hardy, now aged fifty-eight, travelling ever farther afield on his bicycle, visiting such places as Bristol, Gloucester and Cheltenham, sometimes in company with Emma, and at others with his brother Henry. Often, he would take his bicycle part-way on the train. The advantage for literary people, of possessing a bicycle was that they could travel a long distance on it, 'without coming in contact with another mind, not even a horse's...'. In this way there was no danger of dissipating one's mental energy. [12.7]

That February, he wrote an amusing letter to Elspeth Thomson (sister of the artist Winifred Hope Thomson), thanking her for her 'charming Valentine', which made him feel young again. 'I can just remember the time,' said Hardy, 'when written Valentines were customary, before people became so idle as to get everything, even their love-making, done by machinery!' [12.8]

In April, Hardy wrote to poet and critic Edmund Gosse to tell him of a local belief 'still held in remote parts hereabouts', that in the early hours of every Christmas morning, the farm cattle kneel down (as if in prayer). [12.9] The same month, another amusing letter was sent by Hardy to his sister Katharine. Ever one for a good story, Hardy had enquired of a London 'omnibus conductor', how it was that young women who rode their bicycles recklessly into the midst of traffic, did not meet with accidents. 'Oh nao (no); their sex pertects (protects) them', came the reply. 'We dares not drive over them wotever they do; and they do jist wot they likes... No man dares to go where they go.' [12.10] In May, Hardy went to see Mr Gladstone, the former prime minister, lying in state in Westminster Hall, close to the Houses of Parliament 'where his voice had echoed for fifty years.' [12.11]

In July, Hardy, in a letter to Florence Henniker, described a visit to Gloucester Cathedral, where the Perpendicular style of architecture was invented. 'You can see how it [the idea for the Perpendicular] grew in the old [former day] masons' minds,' he said. In September, he told her that the Americans who used to rent a house and 700 acres of shooting near Coniston (presumably the town in the Lake District, and not, as Hardy states, in Lancashire), did so NOT to shoot, 'but to keep the birds from being shot – a truly charming intention.' [12.12]

A letter to William Archer, critic and journalist, revealed Hardy's total disillusionment with the critics. By attempting 'to deal honestly and artistically with the facts of life,' he said, he was liable 'to be abused by any scamp who thinks he can advance the sale of his paper by lying about one.' [12.13] In a witty ending to a letter to Edmund Gosse in December, Hardy advanced the view that that person's poems lacked 'the supreme quality of their author being dead' or alternatively, 'starving in a garret.' [12.14] Whoever said that Hardy lacked a sense of humour?

 ♋

In December 1898, a volume of fifty or so of Hardy's *Wessex Poems* were published by Harper & Brothers. In the main, they were written either in the 1860s, or in recent times after a long lull. They were generally well received; some were about the Napoleonic era, others were drawn from Wessex life. However, the most interesting were those which gave insight into Hardy's state of mind during this period.

Over and over again, the personal poems amongst them show Hardy's regret for lost love. In 'The Temporary the All', he talks of 'fellowship', but also of 'divergence': 'Change and chancefulness in my flowering youthtime,/ Set me by sun near to one unchosen;/ Wrought us fellowlike, and despite divergence,/ Fused us in friendship.'

In 'Hap', he mentions 'suffering', and 'love's loss' specifically, and implies that this, to 'some vengeful god', is a source of revenge (for what?) and amusement: 'If but some vengeful god would call to me/ From up the sky, and laugh: "Thou suffering thing,/ Know that thy sorrow is my ecstacy,/ That thy love's loss is my hate's profiting"'!

In 'Neutral Tones', he looks back to when they (presumably he and Emma), as though 'chidden (scolded) by God', stood by a pond one winter's day, to the present, since when there have been 'keen lessons that love deceives...' and the sun is scathingly referred to as 'God-curst'.

In 'To an Outer Nature', he is resigned to the fact that there will be no re-awakening of his early love: 'Show thee as I thought thee/ When I early sought thee...', he pleads, only to declare that 'Thy first sweetness, Radiance, meetness, None shall re-awaken'.

In 'Revulsion', however, all hope appears to have been extinguished, only agony and disappointment prevail: 'Let me then never feel the fateful thrilling/ That devastates the love-worn wooer's frame,/ The hot ado of fevered hopes, the chilling/ That agonises disappointed aim!/ So I may live no junctive law fulfilling,/ And my heart's table bear no woman's name.' The very title of this poem, and its sentiments, reveal the overwhelming bitterness and disillusionment which Hardy felt in his heart at this time.

In 'At an Inn', Hardy longs to put the clock back, and appears to blame the 'laws of men', presumably the marriage laws, in part for his predicament: 'As we seemed we were not/ That day afar,/ And now we seem not what/ We aching are./ O severing sea and land,/ O laws of men,/ Ere death, once let us stand/ As we stood then!' Finally, in 'I look Into My Glass', Hardy expresses the fervent wish that his heart (desires and longings) had shrunk, just as his wasted skin of age had.

The depth of sentiment expressed in these poems, and the repetitive nature of their themes, leads on to the inexorable conclusion that in them, Hardy is expressing his internal turmoil and sorrow over the failure of his relationship with Emma.

13

A New Century: *Poems of the Past and the Present*: *The Dynasts*: *Time's Laughingstocks*

In London as usual with Emma, in the spring of 1899, Hardy continued to fraternise with the literary set and met with the poet A.E. Housman for the first time. That October he was present in Southampton on the occasion of the departure of troops for the South African War, and saw similar preparations being made by the battery stationed at Dorchester. These events inspired him to write several poems.

In June, Hardy wrote from London to his sister Katharine ('Kitty') asking her to remember to instruct the local carpenter to erect a cupboard outside the door of the bedroom that used to be his study, and he enclosed a diagram showing exactly where this cupboard was to be located. [13.1] He was now writing frequently to Florence Henniker. In July, he complained to her that one of the problems with life in the country was the lack of availability of good music. In October, he told her (referring to the South African War) how he deplored the fact that civilised nations had learnt no other way of settling disputes than 'the old and barbarous one' (presumably, of going to war). In November, he sent her his newly composed sonnet entitled, 'The departure of the Battery'. [13.2]

〰️

The coming of the new century in 1900 saw Hardy as energetic as ever; cycling from Max Gate all the way to Portland Bill and back in one day; a distance of 20 miles, up hill and down dale. That February, he expressed to Florence Henniker his enjoyment in studying the strategy and tactics of war, but his horror at the fate of Boer General Piet Cronje, whose army including their womenfolk was currently trapped in a river bed (by British forces), and whose animals were 'mangled'. [13.3]

In July, Hardy appraised William Earl Hodgson, journalist and author, of his view that the (British) Constitution 'has worked so much better under queens than kings, and recommended that the Crown should therefore, by rights, descend from woman to woman! [13.4] In October, he enquired of Florence Henniker whether she had heard from her father, the colonel, currently serving in South Africa with the army. The 'present condition of the English novel,' he declared, 'is due to the paralysing effect of English criticism on those who would have developed it...'. [13.5] In the same month, Emma heard that her sister, Helen, now resident at Lee-on-Solent in Hampshire, had fallen ill. To her credit, Emma left Max Gate immediately to go and look after her. Two months later, however, Helen died at the age of sixty-three.

In April 1901, Hardy is to be seen mourning the death of a favourite cat, which was 'mutilated by the mail train...', even though the railway line was ¼ mile distant from the house. This was Hardy's own cat; the first he had ever had, and he blamed himself for letting it stay out at night. [13.6]

In May, a literary society called the 'Whitefriars Club' did Hardy the honour of visiting him at Max Gate. His mother, who was now aged eighty-eight, got to hear of the visit and was taken by her daughters Mary and Katharine, in her wheelchair (for she was now unable to walk), to witness the carriages conveying the literary society members on their way. How proud she must have felt of her now famous son! [13.7]

In November, Hardy remarked that the army had obtained possession of a part of his 'Egdon Heath'; a spot which until now 'had lain untouched since man appeared on the earth!' [13.8]

Poems of the Past and the Present was published in November 1901, by Harper & Brothers of New York. The poems cover a variety of subjects: war, other writers and poets (in particular, Shelley and Keats), flowers, birds, Rome, Switzerland, and there is one humorous poem 'The Ruined Maid'. However, the most profound are those which clearly shed light on Hardy's mental state, even though perhaps he would not have wished the reader to guess that this was the case.

For example, the following are extracts from the poem 'I Said to Love': 'It is not now as in old days/ When men adored thee and thy

105

ways...', and it continues, 'I said to him,/ "We know more of thee than then;/ We were but weak in judgement when,/ With hearts abrim,/ We clamoured thee that thou would'st please/ Inflict on us thine agonies!...".' The poem goes on to refer to 'iron daggers of distress', but says 'We are too old in apathy!' to fear any further threats from 'Love'. The inference is quite clear. Hardy (and Emma) showed poor judgement by marrying each other, and suffered agonies in consequence.

Then there is a heart-rending lament for a lost love entitled 'To Lizbie Browne': 'When, Lizbie Browne,/ You had just begun/ To be endeared/ By stealth to one,/ You disappeared/ My Lizbie Browne!' It continues: 'You were a wife/ Ere I could show/ Love, Lizbie Browne.' Who was Lizbie Browne? Known to Hardy in his youth, she was in fact the beautiful, red-headed daughter of a gamekeeper. The inference is obvious. Hardy in retrospect, felt that it was she he should have married. Instead, he let her slip, when he should have 'coaxed and caught' her, ere she passed.

In 'How Great My Grief', Hardy reveals much about the state of his marriage: 'How great my grief, my joys how few,/ Since first it was my fate to know thee!/ – Have the slow years not brought to view/ How great my grief, my joys how few,/ Nor memory shaped old times anew,/ Nor loving-kindness helped to show thee/ How great my grief, my joys how few,/ Since first it was my fate to know thee?'

This is not the voice of a man who cares nothing for his wife, and has moved on and had an affair, in order to achieve happiness. No, this is the voice of utter dejection and resignation. The marriage is over; dead, buried, and for Hardy, time passes slowly. And yet, if there was no hope whatsoever left in Hardy's heart, why would he then still have been writing poems on the subject?

☙❧

The reason that neither Hardy's parents, nor his siblings, ever visited him at Max Gate was apparently that Emma did not welcome them there. According to Hardy's acquaintance, Dorset-born publisher Newman Flower, matters came to a head one day when Hardy, returning from a walk, discovered that a young relative who had been visiting him there, had been 'sent away' (presumably by Emma) during his absence for no reason whatsoever. This action at last aroused Hardy to anger, and he resolved to live his future life in his study. To this end, he consulted a builder, with a view to building a stairway to his study from the garden, so that he might avoid having to go through the house to reach his room. 'He would have all his meals in his room. He would live there.' [13.9]

$$\sim\!\!\bigcirc\!\!\sim$$

On New Year's Eve 1901, Hardy made a profound statement regarding how an individual is to determine his own philosophy of life. 'Let every man make a philosophy for himself out of his own experience', was Hardy's advice. It was impossible to avoid using the 'terms and phraseology' of earlier philosophers, but 'if he values his own mental life', then he should 'avoid adopting their theories'. Years of labour could be avoided by working out one's views as given by one's surroundings. Say one adopted a pessimistic standpoint, for example; in Hardy's opinion, this was the only view of life in which one can never be disappointed. 'Having reckoned what to do in the worst possible circumstances...', then, 'when better arise, as they may, life becomes child's play.' [13.10]

In February 1902, Hardy lamented the fact that 'Theological lumber' was still being allowed to discredit religion. If the Church were to replace 'the doctrines of the supernatural', by 'reverence and love for an ethical ideal', then the great majority of thinking people who hitherto had been 'excluded by the old teaching' would be brought back into the fold and 'our venerable old churches and cathedrals would become the centres of emotional life that they once were.' [13.11]

That April, Hardy wrote to Dr Elias Kerr, physician of Dorchester, to complain that visitors to the town were unable to find various streets and 'spots' (places) on account of their names having been changed, and put forward certain suggestions as to how this could be rectified. This included the use of inscribed stone tablets to mark the former sites of The Old Theatre; the Gallows; the Romano-British burial ground; the Franciscan Friary; and Dorchester Castle. [13.12]

In May, to celebrate the peace agreement signifying the end of the Boer War, Hardy flew a flag (presumably the Union flag) in the garden of Max Gate. [13.13] That September, Hardy remarked on how motor-cars were 'rather a nuisance to humble roadsters (Hardy was still relying on his bicycle, and did not yet possess a car) like me', as one never knew whether their occupants were 'Hooligan-motorists or responsible drivers.' [13.14]

❧

During the latter part of 1902, Hardy was working on volume one of *The Dynasts*; a story which had been taking shape in his mind over a number of years. For this he moved location yet again within Max Gate, into a newly-constructed study above a new kitchen. The extra space provided by the extension enabled Emma to commandeer the two attic rooms on the second floor, to which she withdrew for long periods and spent her time reading, sewing and painting.

❧

In January 1903, Hardy remarked upon 'the decay of Parliamentary government', a sentiment which might apply equally well today! The problem could be solved, he said, by 'electing a wise autocrat', and 'conceding to him unlimited sway (authority) for a fixed term.' [13.15]

The following month, Hardy was advising caution in the treatment of an ancient building, in this case, the tower of Fordington Church, which he described as a 'venerable monument', much admired by the famous architect Sir Gilbert Scott. [13.16] Hardy was currently complaining of rheumatism, and Emma was 'ailing'. Both were suffering from lassitude. [13.17] In April, Hardy expressed his view on capital punishment, admitting that it was a deterrent, but questioning 'the moral right of a community to inflict that punishment...'. [13.18] In June, Emma was obliged to leave London for Dorset, having 'contracted a severe cough almost on the day of her arrival.' Hardy attributed this to the wet and cold weather. By July, because she had not recovered, Hardy returned to Max Gate. [13.19]

In September, Hardy gave his view on the subject of vivisection, which he felt was a small matter in comparison with 'the general cruelty of man to the "lower" animals'. Perhaps if, say, the lions had won the upper hand instead of the human race, then, 'they would have been less cruel by this time.' In his view of lions, Hardy was mistaken; they are not 'cruel' in the sense that they indulge in gratuitous torture, (like one of Hardy's favourite animals, the cat!), or kill for the sake of killing (like the fox), but rather, being carnivorous, they are obliged to kill in order to survive. [13.20]

In January 1904, the first volume of *The Dynasts* was published by Macmillan.

∾

In 1904, Hardy was introduced to a twenty-five-year-old schoolteacher, literary critic, and published author of children's books who was a long-standing admirer of his works. This was Florence Emily Dugdale, who would one day play a pivotal role in his life. How this meeting came about is unclear, but as Florence Henniker was present at the time, it may be that the two Florences were friends. Not being in the best of health, Florence Dugdale was seeking an alternative and less arduous occupation to teaching. This Hardy was able to provide, by enlisting her support in helping him research his books.

In March, Hardy said he found it difficult, with his limited knowledge of the subject, to pronounce on which 'sport' was the most cruel. However, those who derived pleasure from watching an animal struggling to 'escape the death agony' which was deliberately inflicted on it by human beings, was to his mind 'one of the many convincing proofs that we have not yet escaped from barbarism'. [13.21]

Hardy's mother, Jemima, died on April 3, 1904, which was Easter Sunday. She was buried at Stinsford in the same grave as her husband. Although ninety years of age, her memory and intellect had remained undimmed. 'It took me hours to be able to think and express what she had at the tip of her tongue,' said Hardy. The gap left by her departure was 'wide, and not to be filled'. [13.22] Mary, Katharine and Henry Hardy attended the funeral, but significantly, Emma stayed away.

The following month Hardy reported on the loss of his oldest friend in Dorchester, the historian, antiquarian, and water-colour artist Henry Moule. Moule's friendship with Hardy was a true friendship 'which many waters cannot quench, nor the floods drown'. [13.23]

Hardy's letter-writing continued unabated throughout the years. In July, he was complaining to Alfred Pope, brewer, and former Mayor of Dorchester, about odours emanating from the town's sewage system; which were so foul that he felt unable to invite friends down to Max Gate. [13.24] In October, he informed Edmund Gosse of the death of

Emma's brother Walter, assistant manager of a general post office, who had retired only six months previously.

In April 1905, Hardy at last steeled himself to make the long journey up to Aberdeen in Scotland, to receive from the university of that city the honorary degree of Doctor of Laws. In May, he attended a farewell banquet to London's Lord Mayor, and went to the theatre to see plays by Ben Jonson and Bernard Shaw. In June, he visited his old friend, the poet Swinburne.

In September a party of two hundred members of the Institute of Journalists visited Hardy at Max Gate, and were provided with tea served from a marquee 150 foot long; the latter having been erected on the lawn especially for the purpose. Visiting Hardy was the members' own idea. Having been the victim of no small amount of criticism from some of their number over the years, he may not have shared their enthusiasm!

In November, displaying his usual attention to detail, Hardy recorded the order in which the trees were shedding their leaves that year, this being: 'Chestnuts; Sycamores; Limes; Hornbeams; Elm; Birch; Beech.' [13.25]

ତ⊙

February 1906 saw the publication of the second volume of *The Dynasts*. In London again that year, Hardy commented that he preferred 'late Wagner (the composer)', just as he also preferred, 'late Turner (the painter)'. As usual, time was spent at the British Museum Library verifying the facts for the final volume three of *The Dynasts*.

In June, Hardy wrote to Captain G.L. Derriman, Secretary of the Royal Society for the Prevention of Cruelty to Animals, stating that he feared that the rabbits, pigeons and other birds featured in a conjuring performance at London's Alhambra Theatre, may possibly have been 'drugged or blinded to make them passive...'. [13.26] Here, Hardy was again ahead of his time.

In August, he and his brother Henry went on a cycling tour to visit the cathedrals of Lincoln, Ely and Canterbury; and also the Cambridge colleges. Henry was then aged fifty-five, whereas Hardy was eleven years older; so this was no mean feat for a man of his age!

In February 1907, Emma went to London to join the suffragist procession (believers in rights of women). Hardy was himself in favour of

Thomas Hardy in 1906.
Photo: Dorset County Museum.

women's suffrage, as stated in a letter to the leader of its movement, Millicent Fawcett. [13.27] The following month the couple met playwright George Bernard Shaw and his wife Charlotte, it is believed for the first time. [13.28] In June, they attended a garden party given by King Edward VII at Windsor Castle. Now Hardy had truly 'arrived' in society, whether he liked it or not! In November, the Dorsetshire Regiment, then based in India, asked him to provide them with a marching tune; it must have local affinities, and be suitable for rendition with fifes and drums. He duly obliged with an old tune of his grandfather's called 'The Dorchester Hornpipe'.

In March, Hardy wrote to Florence Dugdale, advising her not to carry out searches (which she was doing on his behalf for *The Dynasts*) in the British Museum if she was 'not quite well'. He also suggested that she demand the sum of 21 guineas, rather than the £8 proposed, for the children's stories which she was writing. [13.29] In April, Hardy asks if 'Miss Dugdale' can be away from school for a day to join him in another search, this time at the South Kensington Museum. (At the time, Florence was a teacher at St Andrew's National School, Enfield, Middlesex, where her father was headmaster.) [13.30]

In July, Hardy wrote an introductory letter to publisher Maurice Macmillan, recommending Florence to be an assistant to his firm 'in the preparation of school books and supplementary readers.' [13.31] (Macmillan had previously published Hardy's *The Woodlanders*, and *Wessex Tales*, and were currently engaged in publishing *The Dynasts*; the third and last volume of which appeared in February 1908.)

☙

The Dynasts: A Drama of the Napoleonic Wars, in Three Parts, Nineteen Acts, and Thirty Scenes, is the longest dramatic composition in English literature. It is an historical narrative, written mainly in blank verse, but also in other metres and in prose; and centres around the tragic figure of Napoleon. It begins in 1805, with Napoleon's threat to invade England; covers the Battle of Trafalgar; the war in the Spanish Peninsula; Napoleon's Russian campaign; and finally the battle of Waterloo, where the great French commander is defeated by Napoleon. Although *The Dynasts* was a play, said Hardy, it was 'intended simply for mental performance, rather than for production on the stage of a theatre.

There are many informative scenes: a debate in the House of Commons, Napoleon's coronation, Napoleon's divorce of Josephine and his marriage to Marie Louise, and so forth; featuring many characters: amongst them, Lord Nelson and William Pitt. However, it may be argued that of even greater importance are the 'Spirits' – which Hardy describes as 'supernatural spectators of the terrestrial action...'. They include the Spirit of the Years, of the Pities, of Rumour, and the Spirits Sinister and Ironic. The 'Shade of the Earth' and the 'Angels' provide the choruses.

In his Preface, Hardy describes *The Dynasts* as 'the Great Historical Calamity, or clash of Peoples, artificially brought about some hundred years ago.' (His view of the conflict as a 'Tragedy' was probably at variance with the vast majority of English people, who would have seen Napoleon's defeat as a cause for celebration.)

His 'Spirits' appear to reflect the various viewpoints of a 'normal' onlooker to what is happening on the earth below; rather than having any religious connotation. The doctrines of the Spirits however, 'are but tentative', and not intended to offer the reader a 'systematized philosophy' which might explain the mystery of 'this unintelligible world'. [13.32] In Hardy's words, the existence of these external features, the Spirits and the Choruses, were 'shaped with a single view to the modern expression of a modern outlook...'.

Was it possible, from a study of Napoleon, to draw some general conclusions about life on earth, and shed light on the great unanswered questions of the 'Why' and the 'Wherefore'? The very fact that Hardy's 'Spirits' reflect different perspectives (appropriate to their various titles) would appear to make the discovery of any coherent rationale to explain the observed facts impossible!

Is it given to us, to anyone, to understand 'this unintelligible world'? In *The Dynasts*, Hardy postulates the existence of an 'Immanent (all-pervading, universal) Will'. The words: 'This Tale of Will/ And life's impulsion by Incognizance', sums up the situation perfectly. The peoples of the earth are being continually pushed hither and thither, by some great force – which he calls the 'Urging Immanence' [13.33] – of which they are completely unaware. Hence Hardy's comment that the Napoleonic Wars were brought about 'artificially'.

Despite his protestations to the contrary, Hardy has provided an explanation for life on earth, i.e. that we are being manipulated by an external force, without our knowledge. The corollary to this is that everything we experience is predetermined. What motivates this 'Will', and what its values are, if any, and where it has its origins, is not explained, except to say that it 'reasonest not...' and is both 'Loveless' and 'Hateless' at the same time! [13.34] The fact that it drove Napoleon to fight Wellington, the Prussians and the Russians, and vice-versa, suggests that it may even have a malicious, destructive component.

The Dynasts does end on a note of hope: '... the rages/ Of the ages/ Shall be cancelled', the Chorus sings out; '...deliverance', it says, will be 'offered from/ the darts that were...', so that, 'Consciousness the Will informing...' will finally '... fashion all things fair.' In other words, the 'Will' will make itself known to man, and all will be made well.

Hardy seems to be saying that, until the universal 'Will' makes itself known to us, it is not possible for us to understand why things happen, and acting, in his words like 'puppets', 'the mindless minions of the spell' [13.35], we will continue to become enmeshed in events not of our choosing, such as war.

☙

In 1908, Hardy was as active as ever, receiving a visit from Lady St Helier, dining at the Royal Academy, attending a performance of some scenes from *The Dynasts* by a Dorchester dramatic society, visiting Cambridge, and attending the Mansion House for a dinner commemorating the poet John Milton. However, because Emma felt 'too weak to undertake housekeeping up there', the Hardys did not rent accommodation in London that year, as was their usual practice. [13.36]

In September, Hardy wrote at length about 'Marky', a favourite cat, who in the process of making a bed for her forthcoming kittens, had visited the bedroom of Jane, one of the Max Gate servants, and 'torn her Sunday hat in rents...'. The hat cost 4s/11d, said Hardy, who gave her 5s/- to buy another, 'and she is quite content'. When Marky duly had her kittens, Hardy stated that all but one were to be drowned the following morning. This may at first seem out of character for a professed animal lover such as himself. Nevertheless, it reflects the practicalities of country living. [13.37] Having been nursed by her companion, 'Daisy' until she got over the loss of her kittens, Marky, having made a full recovery from her grief, excelled herself

114

a month later by catching a leveret, which the Hardys cooked and ate. [13.38]

The following month, Hardy expressed his displeasure at the third 'restoration' of Stinsford church, which had occurred 'possibly about 1880'. The net result was that the raising of the roof thereby dwarfed the tower – 'a lamentable proceeding altogether.'

In January 1909, Hardy admitted that while writing *The Dynasts*, he had had 'periodic frights', lest he should not have lived to complete the book. Then, 'alas', he 'rattled along too hurriedly (with the writing of it)'. [13.39] This sentiment will ring a bell with any author over the age of about sixty-five! That year, Hardy was appointed Governor of Dorchester Grammar School. When his friend, the poet Algernon Swinburne died, Hardy's rheumatism prevented him from attending the funeral, which was on April 15. He deplored the attitude of the country to Swinburne's death, describing it as 'ignoring and almost contemptuous.' That autumn, Hardy visited more cathedral cities, this time Chichester, York, Edinburgh and Durham.

On April 25, Hardy was advising the Stinsford church restoration committee. 'The only legitimate principle for guidance,' he said, was to limit all renewals to 'repairs for preservation, and never to indulge in alterations.' This was an interesting building, 'and one very easy to injure beyond remedy.' He gave detailed instructions to the committee, and included a sketch to illustrate how the replacement guttering should be applied. He could not help commenting however, on how the erection in about 1870, of the 'imitation Early English nave roof ... in place of the good old sixteenth-century waggon roof with bosses, which had become decayed...', had irrevocably altered the relation of tower to nave. Not only that, the 'Cholmondeley monument' (to Marcia Cholmondeley, a member of the Pitt family), had been destroyed to create a corbel. [13.40]

In May 1909, Hardy spoke of the good that he believed would come if women were to be given the vote. They would then help abolish blood sports 'slaughter house inhumanities', and the 'present blackguard treatment of animals generally...'. Also, men would then feel free to knock down or rationalize 'all superstitious institutions' such as 'theologies, marriage, wealth-worship, labour-worship', and 'hypocritical optimism...'. [13.41]

In November 1909, in a letter to Florence Henniker, Hardy confessed to being 'not in the brightest of spirits...'. But, 'who can expect to be at my age,' he said, 'with no children to be interested in.' [13.42]

☙

Time's Laughingstocks was a collection of poems by Hardy, some dating back to the mid-1860s. A variety of topics are represented: 'The Fiddler', 'The Dead Quire' (in memory of those who used to sing and play in Stinsford church), 'Former Beauties' (remembering the 'young things ... we loved in years agone'). But, as always with Hardy, it is the personal poems which hold the greatest fascination:

'Bereft' talks of 'my lone bed...'; 'The Dead Man Walking' begins, 'They hail me as one living/ But don't they know/ That I have died of late years,/ Untombed although?'; 'The Division' speaks of '...our severance...', '...that thwart thing betwixt us twain/ Which nothing cleaves or clears...'; and 'He Abjures Love', enquires '... after love what comes?... A few sad vacant hours,/ And then, the Curtain.' The inference is obvious. Although Emma is still alive, Hardy himself feels that as far as he is concerned, he might as well be dead.

There is one poem that alludes to the possibility that there may be a reason for Emma's inability to make him happy. 'The Sigh' declares, 'Not that she (Emma) had ceased to love me/ None on earth she set above me/ But she sighed.' It continues, 'She could not disguise a passion/ Dread or doubt, in weakest fashion/ If she tried...'. Then come the intriguing phrases, 'so I wondered/ Why she sighed.' followed by, 'And she loved me staunchly, truly,/ Till she died;/ But she never made confession/ Why, at that first sweet concession,/ She had sighed.' In other words, although Emma conceded that she loved Hardy, she never explained to him why she sighed, though he does mention some 'sad thought she was concealing...'. (Even though Hardy writes as if Emma were dead, she was in fact still alive when he wrote this poem.) *Time's Laughingstocks* was published by Macmillan in December 1909.

So what was this 'sad thought' that even Hardy was not privy to? In order to try to establish what it may have been, it is necessary to examine the life of Emma Hardy in more detail.

Emma Lavinia Hardy:
The Death of Emma

In addition to the sexual problems experienced by Hardy during his marriage to Emma, there are signs that in other respects, all was not well. Time and again in his writings, Hardy alludes to the fact that Emma is in his view, suffering from some kind of personality disorder. For example, in 'You Were the Sort that Men Forget' (in which he refers presumably to Emma)' he admits that, although he does not include himself as one who has forgotten (her), nevertheless her failings, in his view, were considerable. The poem describes how, by her inept words, she offended people; and how she 'lacked the eye to understand.../ Those friends...' whose dim purport (intention), even though seemingly crude and offhand 'Outpriced the courtesies of the bland.'

In 1894, Hardy revealed his fascination with the subject of the relationship between the sexes when he made certain annotations in the margins of a book entitled *Keynotes*, given to him by Florence Henniker. Beside a passage describing 'the eternal wilderness, the untamed, primitive, savage temperament that lurks in the mildest, best woman', Hardy wrote: 'This if fairly stated is decidedly the UGLY side of a woman's nature.' Where the book refers to man's 'chivalrous, conservative devotion to the female idea he has created, (which) blinds him, perhaps happily, to the problem of her complex nature', Hardy wrote 'ergo

Emma Lavinia Hardy.
Photo: Dorset County Museum.

(therefore): REAL woman is abhorrent to man? hence the failure of matrimony??' This is a desperately negative view, but it should be remembered that although Hardy fell in love many times in his youth, and probably thereafter, his only intimate experience with a member of the opposite sex may well have been his relationship with Emma. [14.1]

In March 1914, sixteen months after Emma's death, Hardy, in a letter to Florence Henniker, refers to Emma's latter years as a time when her 'mind was a little unhinged at times, and she showed unreasonable dislikes.' [14.2] In November he states, also in Emma's latter years, that 'an unfortunate mental aberration for which she was not responsible (had) altered her much, and made her cold in her correspondence with friends and relatives...' which was 'contrary to her real nature.' [14.3]

In his poem 'The Interloper', Hardy recreates his early courting days at St Juliot in the 1870s. Its subtitle 'And I saw the figure of Madness seeking for a home', lends weight to the theory that, in Hardy's mind, Emma was mad. More specifically, there are references to 'a hollow voice' at a dinner party, which he would 'fain not hear...'; to a crowd, enjoying themselves on a lawn 'save one, mirthless,/ Who ought not to be there.'; and to a person 'under which (even the) best lives corrode;/ Would, would it could not be there!' In other words, Emma's presence, mirthless and corrosive, was a huge embarrassment to Hardy when the couple were in company. Was Hardy the only person to notice something strange about Emma, or had others noticed it also? The answer is a most emphatic, yes.

Emma's disdain for Hardy was well known. In 1895, referring to her husband, she told Edward Clodd that 'A man who had humble relations shouldn't live in the place where he was brought up.' [14.4] Some years later, Emma, with Hardy's relatives in mind, referred scathingly to 'the peasant class'. [14.5] Author Mabel Robinson, writing about Emma in the spring of 1891, said that her 'thoughts hopped off like a bird on a bough...'. [14.6]

Christine Wood Homer, a friend of the Hardys, was able to shed even more light on the personality of Emma. If a visitor arrived at Max Gate, and Emma suspected that the visitor had 'no interest in or friendship for her, but had come only to see Mr Hardy and worship at his shrine', she would not inform her husband of the presence of that visitor, who would go away 'without seeing his hero'. Emma 'would have liked to have received the admiration of the world for talents she believed she possessed, but which were not discernible to anyone else'. However, according to Mrs Wood Homer, the poems Emma wrote were 'indifferent', and as for her talents, they were 'not discernable to anybody else.'

One day, when Christine Wood Homer was a girl, Emma arrived at her house and asked if she might see her pet rabbits, guinea pigs, and birds. Instead of looking at any of the animals, Emma 'spent the whole time watching the flies on the window panes...' and expressing 'enthusiastic delight at the sweet way in which they washed their little faces and stroked their pretty wings.' When Christine was aged sixteen, Emma asked her if she would like to accompany her by train on a visit to Parkstone to see a friend, who had 'an aviary of foreign birds' in her garden. They arrived at the friends house and viewed the birds together. Then Emma, ignoring Christine altogether, withdrew to the drawing-room where she and her friend read poetry to one another. When it was time to catch the train home, Emma travelled first class, and left Christine to travel third class.

Christine states that Emma 'had the fixed idea that she was the superior of her husband in birth, education, talents, and manners. She could not, and never did, recognise his greatness.' Also, it had been 'a burdensome grief' to Hardy, that Emma 'had not cared for any of his family.' In summary, Christine described Emma as 'a peculiar woman, and in many ways like a little child...' but whereas at first 'she had only been childish, with advancing age ... (she) became very queer and talked curiously.' [14.7]

It was not only friends, aquaintances and employees who remarked on Emma's bizarre behaviour, but also her relations. Leonie Gifford, Emma's second cousin, visited Emma in 1910, on an occasion when a visitor of some importance was expected for tea but failed to arrive. Despite this, however, Leonie was offered nothing herself. [14.8]

Lorna Heenan was the daughter of Dr F.B. Fisher, who (until he retired in 1910) was Hardy's medical adviser. Lorna states that Emma's 'mental condition progressively deteriorated, with a consequential increased strain on her husband.' Also that her '"heretical" outbursts in the local papers caused her husband great embarrassment.' [14.9]

Evelyn Evans was the daughter of Mr A.H. Evans; by day a chemist, but by night, producer of Hardy's plays for the Dorchester Debating, Literary and Dramatic Society. Evelyn, who from an early age had been taught to 'reverence' Hardy, described the 'mauve, satin ribbons' that used to wave from Emma Hardy's bonnet as she bicycled around the town. 'She was considered very odd by the townspeople (of Dorchester),' said Evelyn, who would 'touch their foreheads significantly as she went by, free-wheeling ... with her feet off the pedals.' [14.10]

According to Evelyn, during Emma's last years 'her delusions of grandeur grew more marked. Never forgetting (that) she was an Archdeacon's niece who had married beneath her (in this, Emma was referring to her uncle, the Reverend Edwin Hamilton Gifford, Archdeacon of London) she was heard to say in front of guests, "Try to remember, Thomas Hardy, that you married a lady." She persuaded embarrassed editors to publish her worthless poems and intimated that she was the guiding spirit of (in) all Hardy's work.' [14.11]

Florence Emily Dugdale described witnessing a heated quarrel which had occurred between Hardy and Emma on Christmas Day 1910. Hardy wished to take Florence with him to Bockhampton to visit Mary and Katharine. Emma resisted on the grounds that Hardy's sisters would poison Florence's mind against her (Emma). [14.12]

Emma, who donated money to numerous charitable institutions including the Salvation Army, the Evangelical Alliance, and others connected with animal welfare, was in the habit of having pamphlets printed, which she left in shops, or in the homes of people she visited. The purpose of these 'beautiful little booklets', as she described in her own (somewhat ungrammatical) language, was to 'help make the clear atmosphere of pure Protestantism in the land and revive us again in the truth...'. [14.13] As might be guessed, Emma, in her views was a violently anti-Catholic!

In 1911, Emma had privately printed a volume of fifteen of her poems, entitled *Alleys*, and in 1912 a volume of her prose entitled *Spaces*. In the latter, her detailed description of what she envisages the Day of Judgement to be like is, in the words of Hardy's biographer Michael Millgate, 'the product of a mind at once obsessed, muddled, and naive.' [14.14] Professor J.O. Bailey (Professor of English at the University of North Carolina at Chapel Hill, U.S.A.) described *Alleys* as 'the exclamations of a child's pleasure in bird-songs and flowers.' As for *Spaces*; this was 'a day-dream made of scraps from the orthodoxy (which) she opposed to Hardy's agnostic views.' Both *Alleys* and *Spaces* revealed 'a basically healthy faith in life', but they revealed also 'a tendency to confuse fantasy and fact'. [14.15]

Newman Flower regarded this as 'A mild form of religious mania'. Emma became 'eccentric', he said. 'She would leave an open copy of the Bible (permanently) on the dressing-tables of the [her] guests' bedrooms', even though the page might be 'thick with dust before the next visitors arrived...'. [14.16]

Writer A.C. Benson, and poet and critic Edmund Gosse visited Max Gate together in September 1912. Benson described as 'something intolerable', the prospect of Hardy having 'to live day and night with the absurd, inconsequent, puffy, rambling old lady...'.

She [Emma] is so queer, and yet has to be treated as rational, while she is full, I imagine, of suspicions and jealousies and affronts which must be half insane.' Benson also described Emma as 'flighty and peevish...'. While showing Benson around the dining room, Emma talked 'in a low, hurried voice, as if she was thinking aloud and not regarding me at all...'; and in the garden, became absorbed in 'pinching the pods of the 'Noli me tangere' to make them eject their seeds', at which she made 'little jumps' and gave 'elfin shrieks of pleasure'. [14.17]

On December 17, in a letter to Florence Henniker, Hardy made reference to 'certain painful delusions...' which Emma 'suffered from at times'. [14.18] Edward Clodd, for his part, described the 'absurd' way in which Emma dressed, as reminiscent of some nymph in a picture by Botticelli. This is amply borne out by contemporary photographs taken of Emma.

In April 1913, Hardy visited Clodd at his home in Aldeburgh, Suffolk, and spoke further of the delusions which Emma suffered from, about being followed and conspired against. In the opinion of Hardy, this was consistent with there being a 'mad strain' in Emma's family's blood. Hardy also stated that Emma not only believed that she had inspired Hardy's novels, but that she was actually the author of them! [14.19] Referring, in a visit to Max Gate in July that year, to Hardy's brother Henry as 'a well-set, sensible man', and to his two sisters as 'ladylike, refined' and 'well-informed', Clodd remarked on what a shame it was that Hardy had allowed his 'half-mad wife' to forbid them and their mother access to Max Gate. [14.20]

❦

If Emma Hardy were alive today, what would she have to say in her defence? Perhaps her own words should speak for her. Emma described the home in Plymouth where she was brought up as 'a most intellectual one ... (and) one of exquisite home-training and refinement...'. 'Alas,' she said 'the difference the loss of these amenities and gentilities has made to me!' [14.21] (Presumably by this she meant since her marriage to Hardy.) She went on to describe her dancing lessons, and the pretty dresses which she wore to parties at which 'the military and navy [were] usually present...'. [14.22]

In November 1894, Emma complained that Hardy's interest in the cause of women's suffrage was 'nil'. 'He understands only the women he invents [i.e. the characters of his novels], the others not at all'. [14.23] In February 1896, Emma wrote to Hardy's sister Mary, then headmistress of the Bell Street junior school for girls in Dorchester. It was 'entirely your fault,' she said, that Hardy had been 'outrageously unkind to me'. 'Ever since I have been his [Hardy's] wife', said Emma, 'you have done all you can to to make division between us ... [and to] set your family against me...'. It was a 'wicked, spiteful, and most malicious habit' of Mary's to say of people she disliked that 'they are "mad"'. Mary had spoilt not only her life, but also that of her husband. Nevertheless, 'your own punishment must inevitably follow, for God's promises are true for ever'. And she ended 'You are a witch-like creature and quite equal to any amount of evil-wishing and speaking – I can imagine you and your mother and sister on your native heath raising a storm on a Walpurgis night [the eve of the 1 May, when witches convene and hold revels with the devil]'. [14.24]

Another of Emma's fears was that the French would invade England and enforce the Catholic faith. For this reason she always kept with her a suitcase filled with provisions, so that if the necessity arose, she could take flight! [14.25]

By February 1897, Emma's comments about Hardy were becoming increasingly acidulated. 'One thing I abhor about Authors ... [she said] is their blank materialism... I get irritated at their pride of intellect...'. [14.26] By August 1899, a note of bitter resignation had entered into her writings. 'I can scarcely think that love proper, and enduring, is in the nature of men... There is ever a desire to give but little in return for our devotion and affection'. She stressed that 'Interference from others is greatly to be feared – members of either families too often are the cause of estrangement (between couples)'. 'If he [in her case Hardy] belongs to the public in any way, [then] years of devotion [on her part] count for nothing'. [14.27]

In November 1902, Emma, in another reference to Hardy the writer, declared 'I fear I am prejudiced against authors – living ones!'. If unsuccessful, 'they too often wear out other's lives with their dyspeptic moanings ... and if they become eminent they throw their aider over their parapets to enemies below, and revenge themselves for any objections to this treatment by stabbings with their pen!' [14.28]

In April 1910, Emma's comments about Hardy were scathing. 'I have my private opinions of men in general and of him in particular – grand brains – much "power" – but too often, lacking in judgement of ordinary matters – opposed to UNselfishness – as regards themSELVES! – utterly useless and dangerous as magistrates! [which Hardy was] and such offices – and to be put up with [by Emma] until a new order of the universe ARRIVES, (IT WILL)'. [14.29]

It must have been a source of great regret to Emma, who had been brought up in a church-going family and whose mother 'read the Bible with exceeding diligence...', that her husband did not share her beliefs. Nevertheless, her faith was undimmed, for in January 1911 she declared that '... an Unseen Power of great benevolence directs my ways; I have some philosophy and mysticism, and an ardent belief in Christianity and the life beyond this present one...'. 'Outward circumstances are of less importance' she said, 'if Christ is our highest ideal.' [14.30]

☙

Personality disorders often have their roots in late childhood or adolescence, and continue to manifest into adulthood. Psychiatrists are apt to divide such disorders into various categories; though in regard to Emma Hardy's symptoms, it appears that there is considerable overlap between the various types.

The 'paranoid' type is characterised by a distrust of others on the one hand, and an over-inflated trust in their own knowledge and abilities on the other. Close relationships are avoided; the person appears cold and distant, and tends to bear prolonged grudges. The 'antisocial' type is characterised by a lack of conscience. [14.31]

A feature of the 'histrionic' type, is constant attention seeking. The person will interrupt others in order to dominate the conversation, constantly seeks praise, may dress provocatively with outrageous hairstyles or hats to draw attention to themselves; and believes that their relationships with others are more intimate than they really are. Their main idea is that people will only pay attention to them if they behave in an extreme way, and yet their expression of emotion is rapidly shifting and shallow. They may also think eccentrically, fantasise, and daydream, and may exhibit extreme religiosity. Rebelliousness and a failure to conform may also be features. [14.32]

In the 'narcissistic' type (which is closely related to the 'histrionic') the person presents an exaggerated picture of his or her achievements, and expects others to recognise them as such. They have difficulty in making long-lasting relationships, mainly because they are disinterested in the feeling of others. [14.33] In an effort to convince the world 'what a wonderful, kind, caring, compassionate person' they are, they make 'bold pronouncements', exhibit 'gushing empathy', and are to be found sitting on 'many committees for good causes'. [14.34] There is a grandiose sense of self-importance, and an entrenched belief that their 'personal uniqueness' renders them 'fit only for association with people or institutions of rarefied status'. They are arrogant and haughty, and have a lack of empathy with others. [14.35]

In the 'schizoid' type, the person prefers solitary activities, has no close friends or confidants, and has little interest in sexual activity with another person. [14.36] To concentrate for a moment on the latter, as already observed, when Hardy approaches Emma, she constantly rejects his advances, and in his collection of poems entitled *Time's Laughingstocks*, he alludes to this, for example, in 'To Carry Clavel' (presumably Emma), where he says, 'You turn your back, you turn your back.../ And scorn my company.' In 'A Broken Appointment', he goes further, and accuses her of lacking in her 'make [up]/ That high compassion which can overbear/ Reluctance for pure lovingkindness' sake...'. The chilling phrase 'between us lay a sword', from the poem 'To a Sea Cliff', written by Hardy on their honeymoon, suggests that this rejection by Emma was a problem for him right from the beginning of their married life. In fact, it is distinctly possible that their marriage was never consummated.

The 'schizotypal' variety is considered by some to be a mild form of schizophrenia. Here, as well as exhibiting disorders of thought and perception, the individual may also cherish odd beliefs or superstitions.

&

The epithets 'childlike' and 'trusting' were often applied to Emma by those close to her, and this may reflect the fact that Emma was emotionally immature. Such people will 'spend a large proportion of their lives creating situations in which they become the centre of attention' in order it is believed, to counter their own 'low levels of self-esteem and self-confidence'. However, 'the relief is temporary' because 'the underlying problem remains unaddressed'. [14.37] Impressionability and gullibility are also features of histrionic personality disorder. [14.38]

☙

From such a study of the various manifestations of personality disorder, the character of Emma is instantly recognisable; though it must be said that she does not fit into any one particular category, but rather appears to display the symptoms of several. However, human beings are infinite in their variety, and such categorisation was originally created perhaps more for the benefit of the tidy-minded medical profession, than to represent reality in describing a particular personality.

Given that many of Emma's behaviour patterns (as witnessed by various observers) are commensurate with her having a personality disorder, how then can the 'delusions' from which she suffered in later life (as mentioned by Hardy himself), be explained? A delusion is a false personal belief not subject to reason or to contradictory evidence. [14.39] Two common conditions in which delusions are a feature are schizophrenia and manic-depressive disorder.

It has already been remarked that Emma displayed certain characteristics of schizoid personality disorder. However, Emma's symptomatology in her latter years appears also to fit with a diagnosis of 'mania with psychotic symptoms' (psychotic – meaning severe mental disorder or derangement), where 'inflated self-esteem and grandiose ideas' have developed into 'delusions (which may be religious delusions)', and 'irritability and suspiciousness' have developed into 'delusions of persecution'. In a so-called 'manic' episode, the deranged thought processes, coupled with and increased speed of mental activity, may cause the speech of the individual to become incomprehensible. [14.40]

Both schizophrenia and manic-depression are progressive, in the sense that severity of both illnesses increases with time. In the case of Emma, this is demonstrated not only by her behaviour, but also by her mood. Whereas in the early years of her acquaintance with Hardy, she appeared to be reasonably outward looking; later she withdrew more and more into her shell, preferring to stay at home at Max Gate, often in her room, rather than accompany Hardy to London for the season. Either that, or she would choose to return early from the capital, and leave him up there.

᠖᠑

To summarise, it appears to be an evident fact that Emma Hardy's behaviour was typical of a person with a personality disorder, some of the features of which, particularly in her latter years, were typical of both schizophrenia on the one hand, and manic-depressive disorder on the other.

Perhaps one day in the not too distant future, research into genetics will reveal more about the origin of such conditions. In the meantime, as both manic-depression and schizophrenia are known to have a heritable component, it is reasonable to ask whether any of Emma's relations possessed or developed similar tendencies. The answer to this question is also an emphatic 'yes'.

For instance, Emma's eldest brother Richard, died in the Warneford Asylum at Oxford in 1904 at the age of sixty-nine. Although he suffered from chronic Bright's disease (Glomerulonephritis, inflammation of the kidneys), this would not have explained his apparent mental derangement. In 1919, Emma's niece Lilian Gifford (daughter of her brother Walter) was diagnosed with paranoia and admitted to the London County Council asylum at Claybury in Essex, where she remained for over a year. [14.41] Emma's second cousin Leonie Gifford, was reported to have had 'a series of nervous breakdowns', from her forties onwards. [14.42]

᠖᠑

In March 1910, Hardy visited the grave of his friend, the poet Swinburne, on the Isle of Wight, and composed a poem 'A Singer Asleep' in his memory. In May, when he and Emma were in London in a rented flat, the announcement of the death of King Edward VII was made. Advising Lady Grove about her writing, Hardy confessed modestly 'that I am no authority.' He had 'written heaps of ungram-

126

matical sentences', having learnt his grammar by 'general reasoning, rather than by rules.' To Sidney Trist, editor of the publication *Animals' Guardian*, he explained how difficult it was to extend 'the principle of equal justice to all the animal kingdom', when nature herself was 'absolutely indifferent to justice...'. [14.43]

Hardy whose name appeared in the Birthday Honours List that June, went to Marlborough House the following month to be invested with the Order of Merit by the new King, George V. When Emma returned to Max Gate, Hardy wrote to her saying how depressing it was to come home late in the evening to their 'dark, silent flat', which was 'full of the ghosts of all those who had visited us there.' [14.44] Returning to the subject of suffrage he held that a woman has as much right to vote as a man, but doubted 'if she may not do mischief with her vote.' What the nature of this mischief might be, he did not specify! [14.45]

Thomas Hardy, aged about seventy, by Abrahams.
Photo: Dorset County Museum.

In August, Hardy was complaining to the Superintendent of the Dorchester Police about some boys whom the servants had caught stealing apples from Max Gate. He wished the Superintendent to enquire into the matter, and 'at least caution the boys' (whose names were known to him. However, he did not wish them 'to be punished further', (which presumably would have meant the birch). [14.46]

That November, Hardy was honoured by being given the freedom of his native county town Dorchester. In December, he described as 'such a loss', the death of 'Kitsey' the 'study cat', who was accustomed to sleeping 'on any clean sheets of paper', and 'to be much with me.' [14.47] By this time, Florence Dugdale had become a permanent feature of the Hardy household.

1911 saw Hardy as energetic as ever, continuing with his programme of visits to all the English cathedrals. In April, he was at Lichfield, Worcester and Hereford; and in June with his brother Henry, at Carlisle. This latter visit to the Lake District gave him the opportunity to see the grave of the poet Wordsworth, at Grasmere church, and take in Chester cathedral on the return journey.

In July, this time in company with his sister Katharine, on a visit to Devon, yet another cathedral was ticked off the list, namely Exeter. In November, the Dorchester Debating and Dramatic Society staged performances of plays derived from Hardy's Wessex Novels.

ᏅᎧ

April 1912, saw the sinking of the steamship *Titanic*, which hit an iceberg off the Grand Banks of Newfoundland. This occasioned Hardy to write a poem 'The Convergence of the Twain', in aid of a fund for the victims. This season, instead of renting a flat in London, he and Emma stayed in an hotel.

In June, Hardy was visited at Max Gate by poets Henry Newbolt and W.B. Yeats, who had been asked by the Royal Society of Literature to present him with that Society's gold medal, on the occasion of Hardy's seventy-second birthday. In July, Emma gave what was to be her last garden party, and in August she went on what would be her last visit to the theatre.

On November 22, Emma felt unwell and was obliged to remain upstairs in her bedroom. On the 26th, the doctor called and pronounced that the illness was not of a serious nature. With this news, and with the assent of Emma, Hardy that evening fulfilled a longstanding engagement, by attending the rehearsal of a play by local players in Dorchester. By the time he returned home at 11p.m., Emma was asleep. The following morning, the maid informed Hardy that Emma had seemed brighter, but was now worse. Hardy immediately went to her, and found her lying unconscious. By the time the doctor arrived, she was dead.

Emma was buried in Stinsford churchyard on 30 November; her tomb having been designed by Hardy himself. Rebekah Owen, Hardy's acquaintance from New York, commented on 'the exceeding pathos' of this event, and Rebekah's biographer, Carl J. Weber, pulls no punches when he attributes Rebekah's sentiments on the matter to Emma's 'disdain of what she regarded as the peasant origin of her husband.' [14.48]

A few days before Emma's death, she and Hardy had been involved in a violent quarrel; Emma having ventured into the study into which he had retreated. Hardy believed that this quarrel had contributed to her death, and forever thereafter, he blamed himself for it. [14.49] Soon after Emma's funeral, Hardy discovered in Emma's room, two 'book-length' manuscripts which she had written; one entitled 'The Pleasures of Heaven and the Pains of Hell', and the other 'What I think of my husband'. Having read them he tore out the pages, one by one, and burnt them in the fire that was burning in the grate. [14.50] Hardy also destroyed some 'useless old MSS (manuscripts), entries in notebooks, and marks (footnotes) in printed books.' [14.51]

That same year Henry, Katharine and Mary Hardy, left the family home at Higher Bockhampton (which now reverted to the Kingston Maurward Estate) and moved into a large house Talbothayes Lodge (which had been designed by Hardy in 1893, and built by Henry), situated about a mile east of Max Gate.

Satires of Circumstance, Lyrics and Reveries: Moments of Vision: Late Lyrics and Earlier

Hardy now embarked on poetry writing on a grand scale. In March 1913, he made a nostalgic visit to Cornwall, to St Juliot and other favourite places which he had known with Emma. Calling at Plymouth on the return journey, he arranged for a memorial tablet, designed by himself, to be placed in the church where she had played the organ as a young woman. June found him in Cambridge, receiving the honorary degree of Doctor of Letters, Litt.D.) In July in London, he met Prime Minister Herbert Asquith and his wife Margot.

January 1914 found Hardy engaged in correspondence with the Reverend Cowley, current Vicar of Stinsford, over the retrieval of the church's old font, which had been discovered in the churchyard, buried under some rubbish.

On February 10, 1914, at St Andrew's church, Enfield, Hardy married the thirty-five year old Florence Emily Dugdale. The only other people present, apart from the vicar and an official, were Florence's father and sister, and Hardy's brother Henry. After the ceremony they did not have a honeymoon but returned to Max Gate. Despite the fact of having remarried, Hardy admitted that the 'romance of St Juliot abides none the less, and will if I live to be a hundred.' He derived consolation, however, from the fact that Florence had been 'a great friend of my late wife...', and therefore there

Florence Emily Hardy.
Photo: Dorset County Museum.

would be no 'rupture of continuity', which he so disliked. His ghost, he said, would haunt St Juliot 'by reason of the experiences I was there blest with before my first marriage...'. He evidently regarded Florence as a kindred spirit, and hoped that 'the union of their [his and hers] two rather melancholy temperaments may result in cheerfulness...'. [15.1] It transpired that flower-gardening was a hobby of hers, at which Hardy said she worked 'rather too hard...'. Later he was to describe Florence as a 'tender companion' who was 'quite satisfied with the quietude of life here [at Max Gate].' Theirs was probably not a physical relationship because, as parlour-maid Ellen Titterington states, the couple 'occupied separate bedrooms with a common dressing-room between'. [15.2]

In the spring, Hardy and Florence dined at the Royal Academy, and met with friends before leaving for Cambridge to be entertained by various worthy 'Heads and Fellows' of its university; including Charles Moule (son of the Reverend Henry Moule, vicar of Fordington), formerly tutor of Corpus Christi, whom Hardy had known since his youth. [15.3]

In the summer, the couple motored down to the West Country, Hardy having progressed (if that is the correct word!) from bicycle to car. In fact the car, a 'Benz', was not owned by Hardy (who had never learned to drive), but by Tilley's Garage, in Dorchester, who also provided the chauffeur, Harold Voss. [15.4]

In Plymouth, he took the opportunity to answer questions about the Gifford family vault; an attempt to clear up what he considered to be some loose ends from the past concerning his former wife's ancestors. In June he was again in London, at a dinner of the Royal Institute of British Architects, with which he had kept in touch down the years.

At Max Gate, Hardy enjoyed the company of Wessex, Florence's wire-haired terrier, whom he described as 'spoilt', but nonetheless was 'thriving', and 'fond of other dogs...'. Yes, he said, it would be in order for her to bring her other dog, Milner, to Max Gate also. [15.5] Florence however, worried in case Wessex's barking, and her playing of the pianola, disturbed Hardy in his writings.

In a letter to Florence Henniker in July, he confessed to feeling 'miserable, lest I had not treated her (Emma) considerately in her latter life.'

Having returned from Stourhead in Wiltshire, where they had been guests of Sir Henry and Lady Hoare, Hardy wrote in his diary 'August 4, 11 P.M. War declared with Germany.' Having previously managed to convince himself of 'the gradual bettering [improvement] of human nature', Hardy was now astonished, disillusioned, and depressed at the German invasion of Belgium which had precipitated hostilities. [15.6]

Dorchester would soon be 'teeming with soldiers, mostly drunk...', and Hardy estimated that eventually, one thousand German and Austrian prisoners of war would be confined in Dorchester's artillery barracks. [15.7]

❧

In November 1914, *Satires of Circumstance, Lyrics and Reveries* was published by Macmillan.

'Channel Firing' was a tirade against those who make war in the name of Christ: 'All nations striving strong to make/ Red war yet redder. Mad as hatters/ They do no more for Christe's sake/ Than you do who are helpless in such matters.'

In 'God's Funeral', Hardy indicates his absolute loss of faith. 'Mangled', he says, is 'the Monarch [i.e. God] of our fashioning,/ Who quavered, sank; and now has ceased to be.' And yet there is no joy in this loss, only sadness: '... who or what shall fill his place?' asks Hardy. He sympathised with those who still retained their faith, but confessed 'That what was mourned for, I, too, long had prized.'

Other poems reflect the well known themes. In 'When I Set Out for Lyonesse', Hardy describes the magic that was in his eyes when he first went to Cornwall and met Emma (early hope). In 'The Torn Letter', he admits that now Emma is no more 'That ache for you [i.e. Emma], born long ago,/ Throbs on: I never could outgrow it...' [longing]. 'Why, then, latterly did we not speak [to one another],/ Did we not think of those days long dead, [i.e. that they had shared together]', he asks miserably, in 'The Going' [regret]. How could Emma have known 'That such swift fleeting... would undo me so!', he cries abjectly.

'Rain on the Grave', 'Lament', 'A Dream or No', 'Beeny Cliff', 'St Launce's Revisited', and a host of other such poems reveal the abject misery of the bereaved Thomas Hardy.

Although Hardy often juxtaposes the male and female characters in his poems, the references are nonetheless plain for all to see. 'A plaintive lady pale and passionless...' (from 'The Wistful Lady); 'So came it that our fervours/ Did quite fail/ Of future consummation...' ('The Re-Enactment') reinforces the notion that Hardy's marriage was never physically consummated. 'The Telegram' goes further, describing 'a

132

moment of aversion', which 'mars her [presumably Emma's] recent spousal grace...', and a 'silence', where 'we two sit together in our waning honeymoon', so that for Hardy, all the future holds is 'lovelessness... stretching from the present to the grave...'.

◌◌

Hardy's new life with Florence continued, outwardly at least, in much the same way as it had done with Emma. Studies of philosophy and ethics were intermingled with visits in 1914 by himself and Florence to the West Country, and to London. In December he reported that Wessex had 'developed a tendency to fight other dogs'. Perhaps if he received a nip from the big dog that lived nearby, that would make him 'less bumptious!' [15.8]

◌◌

In 1915 Hardy decided not to have his customary 'season' in London 'owing to the war and other circumstances.' [15.9] In September he learned that a relative of his, a Lieutenant Frank George, had been killed at Gallipoli, bringing the tragedy of war home to him in even sharper relief. In October, in a letter to Charles Gifford, the late Emma's first cousin, Hardy was still desperately trying to piece together Emma's full genealogical family tree.

November 24 saw the death of Hardy's elder sister Mary, who died at his brother Henry's house at Talbothayes. A school-teacher by profession, her hobbies had been portrait painting and playing the organ at local churches, where she was much in demand. Hardy described her as 'almost my only companion in childhood'. [15.10] She was buried at Stinsford.

◌◌

In June 1916, Hardy fulfilled his duty as Grand Juror at the Assizes, and attended rehearsals of scenes from *The Dynasts* by Dorchester's Hardy Players. In the same month he made a nostalgic visit to Sturminster Newton, where he had written *The Return of the Native*.

September saw him and Florence at St Juliot, revisiting the sites of Hardy's early romance with his late wife Emma. Florence appears to have taken this in good part; at any rate, disguising any feelings of

133

jealousy! By autumn, according to Hardy, the number of German prisoners of war at Dorchester had risen to 5000. He paid them a visit, and also visited wounded English servicemen in the local hospital.

૭౨౦

In February 1917, the Commandant of the local prisoner-of-war camp sent some prisoners to Max Gate to root up some trees, so that the kitchen garden could be enlarged. 'Nothing made me feel more sad about the war than the sight of these amiable young Germans', said Hardy [15.11]   In March, Hardy could not contain his indignation at the 'Good-God' theory, which 'after some thousands of years of trial, [had] produced the present and infamous state of Europe (i.e. a Continent ravaged by war)', which Hardy described sarcastically as 'that most Christian Continent!' As for the 'fifty meanings' which attach to the word 'God' he said, the only reasonable one was the 'Cause of Things', whatever that cause may be! His own theory of a 'Goodless-and-Badless God', as portrayed in *The Dynasts*, might, he said, 'perhaps be given a trial with advantage.' [15.12]

In May, Hardy confessed that (owing to poor eye sight, possibly occasioned by the presence of cataracts), he was 'compelled to write by machinery nowadays', a reference to the typewriter. [15.13]

October saw the couple in Plymouth. In November *Moments of Vision and Miscellaneous Verses* was published by Macmillan. Their theme, said Hardy, was to 'mortify the human sense of self-importance' by 'suggesting that human beings are of no matter or appreciable value in this nonchalant universe.' [15.14]

૭౨౦

'Logs on the Hearth' and 'In the Garden' were poems written by Hardy in memory of his sister Mary. In others, such as 'Joys of Memory' and 'To My Father's Violin', Hardy looks back nostalgically at the past; which to him always seems preferable to the present. In the poem 'Great Things', where Hardy admits to a love for 'sweet cider', 'the dance,' 'love', even here he uses the past tense, 'Will always have been great things...', rather than 'are'.

His poems resound with words and phrases such as 'my own heart nigh broke', 'sorrow-wrung', 'mourn'. In 'The Wound' he describes 'that wound of mine...' which had 'pierced me through' yet 'I'd given no sign', in other words, he had kept it to himself. In 'The Blow' he asks, why had someone 'hurled that stone/ Into the sunshine of our [i.e. his and Emma's] days'? And the answer – that 'No aimful author's was the blow [i.e. himself], but it was rather 'the Immanent Doer's [he who appears as the 'Will in *The Dynasts*] That doth not know', who was responsible.

Most people shy away from certain subjects, but Hardy is not afraid to confront the issues: *Moments of Vision* abound with references like 'death', 'mournful mould' (of one deceased), 'tombs' and 'vaults'.

It was Florence Hardy's opinion that there is more of the real Hardy in the poems, than in the novels, and 'Honeymoon Time at an Inn' begs the question, was Hardy talking about himself? What Hardy describes as a 'false dawn' was about to break, and 'two souls' [the honeymoon couple] were lying together, but they were 'opprest', and both confessed to being sad. Suddenly, an 'old-time pier-glass [large mirror]' crashed to the floor and smashed. For the lady, this was a portent of 'years of sorrow'. Surely the mirror's shattered fragments represented Hardy's shattered dreams? And this on day one of his married life to Emma! The inference would appear obvious.

The remainder of *Moments of Vision* deals with the subjects of war and patriotism.

ᖉᕦ

In January 1918, Hardy gave his opinion on the subject of 'pessimism', something of which he had often been accused. 'My motto is, firstly to correctly diagnose the complaint ... and ascertain the cause; then set about finding a remedy if one exists.' [15.15] As for poetry, its glory, he said, lay 'in its largeness, admitting among its creators men of infinite variety.' A measure of his popularity was when such eminent people as Lady Ilchester and Lady Londonderry came to visit him in the spring.

Hardy was now aged seventy-eight. In June, when the Great War was still in progress, he gave a chilling view of what future wars would be like. This one was horrible enough, but would be 'merciful in comparison...' bearing in mind that 'Scientific munition-making is only in its infancy.' [15.16] The war ended at 11a.m. on November 11th of that year.

In February 1919, Hardy signed a petition in support of the establishment for 'the reconstitution of Palestine as a national home for the Jewish people'. In May, he was 'destroying papers [presumably letters and diaries] of the last thirty or forty years...' which, he said, 'raise ghosts'. [15.17]

On his birthday he took Florence and his sister, Katharine, by car to visit one of his favourite places, Salisbury. Soon afterwards, Siegfried Sassoon arrived with a birthday present; a volume of poems from some fifty living poets intended as a 'Tribute'. [15.18] Hardy confessed to Florence Henniker that he would care more about his birthdays if, with every succeeding one, he could see 'any sign of real improvement in the world'. 'All development' was 'of a material and scientific kind...', but despite this 'scarcely any addition to our knowledge was applied to objects philanthropic or ameliorative.' [15.19]

In October, he and Florence attended the Dorchester Assizes, demonstrating Hardy's endless fascination with the legal system and its ramifications. On November 18, the birthday of Thomas Hardy II, he visited his late father's grave.

In December, Hardy opened the Bockhampton Reading Room and Club, which would be that village's memorial to the fallen. In his speech on that occasion, he reminisced about the 'Poor-houses', where parish paupers were accommodated before the workhouses were built.

☙

Accolades now followed thick and fast. In February 1920, Hardy was in Oxford to receive the honorary degree of Doctor of Letters, and also to see a performance of *The Dynasts* by the university players. In March, he was elected honorary fellow of the Royal Institute of British Architects. April saw Hardy visiting London for the last time, when he and Florence attended the marriage of Harold Macmillan to Lady Dorothy Cavendish, at St Margaret's, Westminster. Macmillan's grandfather Daniel (with brother Alexander) had founded the publishing firm of that name (which had published a number of Hardy's works), and his father Frederick, was its chairman. The month of May saw Hardy at Exeter with Florence and Katharine, attending the cathedral service and calling on friends. In a letter to author and critic Harold Child, Hardy admitted to being 'most averse to anything like an interview... and have been for many years.' [15.20]

On April 2, the occasion of Hardy's eightieth birthday, he received a deputation form the Society of Authors, amongst whom was Mr John Galsworthy, whose works Hardy greatly admired. Those who sent congratulatory messages included the King, the Prime Minister, the Vice-Chancellor of Cambridge University, and the Lord Mayor of London! [15.21]

In November, Hardy was expressing a view with which many will identify: that the name 'English', as the name of this country's people, should be insisted upon, and not, 'the vague, unhistoric, and pinchbeck title of 'British'.' [15.22] In December, Hardy modestly described his philosophy merely as 'a confused heap of impressions, like those of a bewildered child at a conjouring show.' [15.23]

That Christmas night, the carol singers came to Max Gate as was the tradition; as did the mummers, who gave a performance of the 'Play of Saint George'. The fact that Hardy 'sat up' to see the New Year in, may perhaps indicate in him a more contented, if not happier frame of mind.

☙

May 11, 1921 saw the death of Charles Moule, the last of the Reverend Henry Moule's seven sons. In June, Hardy and Florence travelled to Sturminster Newton for a performance of 'The Mellstock Quire' in the castle ruins. In July, a company arrived in Dorchester preparing to make a film of *The Mayor of Casterbridge*. In the same month, he attended morning service at Dorchester's church of St Peter; and in July, opened a bazaar in aid of the Dorset County Hospital.

Hardy may have exchanged the bicycle for the motor car, but in other respects his energy, for one of his age, remained prodigious. His letter writing to friends, eminent authors and poets, members of the 'Macmillan' family (his publishers), inquisitive correspondents asking him to explain various aspects of the behaviour of his characters and the supposed locations of his works, distinguished members of universities, the 'Gifford' family, and others was a tour de force.

☙

Late Lyrics and Earlier was published by Macmillan in May 1922. In its

Preface, Hardy expressed his disappointment that the proposed revisions to the Church of England's Book of Common Prayer had not been 'in a rationalistic direction', and according to his wife Florence, from that time onward 'he lost all expectation of seeing the Church (as) representative of modern thinking minds.' [15.24] (In the event, these revisions were rejected by the House of Commons in 1927 and again in 1928.)

The very fact that these poems, unlike many of their predecessors, are less obsessed with 'death' and the nostalgia for past years, indicates that Hardy has now become somewhat less dissatisfied with life. For example, 'This is the weather the cuckoo likes,/ And so do I...' (from 'Weathers'). However, on closer inspection references to well-known themes and problematical conundrums may still be found.

In 'Faintheart in a Railway Train', Hardy speaks of a lost opportunity to introduce himself to a 'radiant stranger' encountered on a station platform. 'The West-of-Wessex Girl' (who from the mention of Plymouth Hoe is apparently Emma) is a poem in which Hardy regrets that she was 'never ... squired ... [attended upon, does he mean, or made love to?]' by him. 'Read by Moonlight', about 'a letter of hers', again, presumably Emma's, speaks of forthcoming 'pain and pine...'.

In 'A Gentleman's Epitaph on Himself and a Lady, Who were Buried Together', Hardy appears to anticipate his own death and burial next to Emma, who is already dead. In this profound poem, Hardy admits that he never kissed her lips, that 'Not a word passed of love [in] all our lifetime ... nor thrill'; that they never had a 'husband-and-wife time [full relationship]'; and that though she was his companion, she was a 'never-known lady' to him.

That Hardy loved Emma, is confirmed in the poem 'The Woman I met', where he speaks of the 'simplicity [which] made me love you... Till I set not Heaven itself above you.' And yet 'despite how I sighed for you;/ So you tortured me, who fain would have died for you!' The very title of 'If It's ever Spring Again' indicates that for Hardy, those happy early days spent with Emma will not come again.

Again and again Hardy, that most stoical individual, reveals how he suffered. 'But she would not heed/ What I melodied/ In my soul's sore need...' he writes in 'Two Serenades', followed by 'Sick I withdrew/ At love's grim hue...'. A poem ironically entitled 'Side by Side', the fright-ful consequences of Hardy's and Emma's union had become apparent.

They were 'estranged'; they had 'not communed/ for many years...'; their hearts were 'distuned'.

'So sank I from my high sublime', says Hardy in 'The Rift', but why? Evidently he himself did not know, for he followed on, 'never I knew or guessed my crime...'. Finally, in total and absolute despair, he agonises over whether it might have been better for him not to have 'pulled this flower [i.e. Emma]/ From the craggy nook it knew,/ And set it in an alien bower...' but rather he should have 'left it where it grew.' ('Fetching Her')

杩

What of Hardy's relationship with the staff at Max Gate? Opinions are mixed. His chauffeur Harold Voss says that he never saw Hardy in a temper. He was a 'real gentleman' who was 'never flurried' but always calm. On the other hand Hardy's gardener Bertie Stephens, who managed the 1-acre garden, conservatory, greenhouse and paddock single-handed, said that 'At no time did Hardy express any appreciation or give any praise for anything that was done...'. Hardy could also 'get into a bit of a mood', and be 'irritable'. Hardy's barber, W.G. Mills of Dorchester, states that Hardy never gave a tip, nor a Christmas present, but was always 'very close with his money'. His cook, Mrs A. Stanley, describes Hardy's trousers as being so worn that they had 'fringes' at their bottoms, 'He was too mean to buy himself a decent pair'. When she made the mistake of giving the postman on Boxing Day 2s/6d on behalf of the family, Hardy refused to reimburse her the money, on the grounds that 'Dorchester people never give tips'. Hardy's cleaner Margaret Male said that Hardy would never acknowledge people who worked for him if he passed them in the street. She attributed this to his shyness. Hardy's parlour-maid Miss Ellen E. Titterington said that although Hardy gave the maids 'quiet little smiles as he passed them on the stairs, he never passed the time of day with them, unless it was to talk about the weather. If she put too much coal on the fire, he would take it off again! Nevertheless, she was prepared to give him the benefit of the doubt. 'The memory of his early days when he was poor,' she said 'must have remained with him and influenced his behaviour.' [15.25]

16

The Famous Tragedy of the Queen of Cornwall: Human Shows, Far Phantasies, Songs, and Trifles: The Death of Hardy

In May 1922, Hardy visited his old home at Higher Bockhampton and was distressed to see that both house and garden had become shabby through lack of care. July brought visits from Florence Henniker, Siegfried Sassoon, Edmund Blunden and E.M. Forster. In August, he cycled with Florence to visit his brother Henry and sister Katharine at Talbothayes Lodge.

In November, Florence Hardy, who by now was answering Hardy's letters on his behalf, wrote to Lady Josephine Sackville, who had requested that Hardy autograph some books for her. The answer was that yes, Mr Hardy was prepared to do so, but only on payment of the fee of half a guinea for each one; the sum of which would be forwarded to the Dorset County Hospital. [16.1]

November 27 was the tenth anniversary of his late wife Emma's death, and he and Florence marked the occasion by placing flowers on her tomb, and the tombs of the other members of the family.

⟡

On April 4, 1923, Florence Henniker died, bringing to an end her thirty-year friendship with Hardy. In May, Hardy was visited by poet Walter de la Mare, and Max Beerbohm (the caricaturist and author) and his wife Florence.

In June, the Hardys visited Oxford and stayed two nights at Queen's College (which made him an Honorary Fellow), calling on the way at Fawley in Berkshire, where his maternal grandmother had lived the first thirteen years of her life as an orphan. In July, Hardy was invited to Dorchester to meet the Prince of Wales (later King Edward VIII), who was there to open a new drill hall for the Dorset Territorial Army, and afterwards the Prince was entertained to luncheon by the Hardys at Max Gate.

In August, Hardy explained why he objected to 'anything like an interview for press purposes.' It was because he had been the victim of 'so much fabrication and misrepresentation in the past...'. [16.2]

⟨◦⟩

On November 15, *The Famous Tragedy of the Queen of Cornwall*, a poetic, one-act play for mummers, was published by Macmillan. Swinburne had already written a romance in couplets on the subject in 1882, but now Hardy himself would bring to life the legendary tale of Tristram, who falls in love with Queen Iseult of Ireland, but actually marries her namesake, Iseult of Brittany.

⟨◦⟩

On December 29, 1923, dramatist George Bernard Shaw and his wife Charlotte visited the Hardys; also Colonel T.E. Lawrence (of Arabia), who had enlisted earlier that year as a private soldier in the Tank Training School at Bovington, under the assumed name of 'T.E. Shaw'. Lawrence lived in a remote cottage called Clouds Hill, which lay 7 miles from Max Gate.

⟨◦⟩

Anniversaries were very important to Hardy, who on April 3, 1924, recorded in his diary, 'Mother died twenty years ago today.' On April 21, Hardy wrote to General John H. Morgan (lawyer and author, who had been involved in the implementation of the disarmament provisions of the Treaty of Versailles, which marked the end of the Great War), expressing the hope that the League of Nations (which had been inaugurated in January, 1920) offered 'a real hope', that 'Principalities and powers will discern more and more clearly that each personality in them stands himself to lose by war...'. He thought it wrong to blame the English, either entirely, or mainly, for the current poverty in Ireland which, he believed, was caused by the temperament of that country's people – whom he considered romantic and generous nonetheless. [16.3]

In July, Oxford's Balliol College Players arrived to perform the Greek tragedy *Oresteia*, in the garden of Max Gate. On December 31, he 'sat up' and heard on the wireless the chimes of Big Ben heralding the New

Year. On July 15 a deputation arrived from the University of Bristol to confer on Hardy the honorary degree of Doctor of Literature. This was the fifth university to honour him in this way. In December, players from London's Garrick Theatre gave a performance of Hardy's *Tess of the D'Urbervilles* in Max Gate's drawing-room.

෴

Human Shows, Far Phantasies, Songs, and Trifles was published on November 20, 1925 by Macmillan. The poems contain a medley of favourite themes; 'The Turnip Hoer', 'The Monument Maker', 'A Sheep Fair', 'The Graveyard of Dead Creeds', and so forth; and the majority of them reveal Hardy in a lighter mood than heretofore. However, Emma is never far from his mind, as for instance in 'Last Love-Word', which ends with the couplet 'When that first look and touch,/ Love, doomed us two.' In 'A Second Attempt', he describes a time 'Thirty years after' (which is likely to be a reference to when he first met Emma), when he appears to be attempting to relive his life with her, until finally he realises that in the end it 'Twice-over cannot be!'. In 'A Poor Man and a Lady', Hardy's feelings of inferiority surface once again. After a time of 'timorous secret bliss', they become divided: 'Never a kiss of mine could touch you [presumably Emma]', says Hardy; and his marriage to her, 'A comely woman of noble kith, was therefore, 'not a valid thing...'. 'Known Had I', 'Her Haunting-Ground', 'Days to Recollect' and several other poems reflect remorse and regret for lost life.

෴

On December 23, 1925, Hardy remembered the tenth anniversary of his beloved sister Mary's death in his diary. 'She came into the world ... and went out ... and the world is just the same ... not a ripple on the surface left.' [16.4] This was not strictly true, for apart from anything else, Mary had left some beautiful portraits behind of members of her family, without which our knowledge of them would have been that much the less.

෴

Hardy's letter-writing continued unabated, albeit with the help of

Florence, on whom he relied in this respect because of his failing eyesight. Amongst people with whom he corresponded in 1926 were J.B. Priestley, H.G. Wells, John Galsworthy and and Gustav Holst. He also wrote to Marie Stopes (the Scottish birth-control campaigner); in fact it was a characteristic of Hardy that he liked to associate with avant-garde women!

In January 1926, Hardy relinquished his Governorship of the Dorchester Grammar School. Sitting on committees had never been his favourite pastime; rather than controlling or ordaining the activities of others, he preferred to be 'the man with the watching eye', in other words, one who observes events and records them faithfully. [16.5] February found him entering into correspondence regarding the condition of the bells of Stinsford Church, which had fallen into a sad state of disrepair. [16.6]

In July, he confessed in a letter to his old friend, the author Edward Clodd, his fear that, 'rational religion does not make much (head) way at present.' In fact, the 'movement of thought' appeared to have 'entered a back current in the opposite direction', which was however 'not uncommon in human history.' [16.7]

In September, he received an ovation at the (William) Barnes Theatre in Weymouth, where he was attending a dramatisation of 'The Mayor of Casterbridge'. In November, he and Florence made what was to be his last visit to the old family home at Higher Bockhampton. That same month T.E. Lawrence, of whom Hardy was immensely fond, set out for a new R.A.F posting in India.

On December 23 carol singers arrived at Max Gate (as was traditional), this time from St Peter's Church, Dorchester. On the 27th, the 'devoted and masterful' dog Wessex died. He was buried in the garden, under the trees. Wessex's headstone, designed by Hardy himself, was inscribed with the words, 'THE FAMOUS DOG, WESSEX August 1913-27 Dec. 1926 Faithful. Unflinching'. Hardy also commemorated his dear friend and companion for thirteen years with a poem in which Wessex, in his after-life, was searching in vain for his master. That New Year's Eve, Hardy did not 'sit up' to see the New Year in.

ᏇᏉ

On June 2, 1927, Hardy celebrated his eighty-seventh birthday, not at home, but in Devonshire, in the company of his friends Harley Granville Barker (the actor, producer, dramatist, and critic), and his wife Helen. On July 21, he laid the foundation stone of the new Dorchester Grammar School, an event which would have given one such as he – who cherished education and learning – great pleasure.

In August, Hardy, in company with the composer Gustav Holst, motored to 'Egdon Heath', and visited Puddletown church, where Hardy's ancestors had played in the choir ('quire'). This month and the following brought visits to Bath, Ilminster and Yeovil (in Somerset), Lulworth Castle and Charborough Park.

Although at the end of October he and Florence took a short stroll across the fields from Max Gate, from now on Hardy depended on being driven by chauffeur in his hired car, which took him to Stinsford (to put flowers on the family graves), and to Talbothays (to see brother Henry and sister Katharine).

On Armistice Day, November 11 (the ninth anniversary of the end of the Great War), Hardy and Florence listened to the service of thanksgiving, broadcast on the wireless from Canterbury cathedral. [16.8] Thursday, November 24, and Sunday, November 27, marked the anniversaries of the deaths of sister Mary and first wife Emma respectively; Hardy wore a black hat, and carried Emma's black walking stick as tokens of his mourning.

Over the years, it had been Hardy's habit to sit at his 'writing-table' every morning at 10a.m. If the spirit moved him, he would write; if it did not, he would find something else to do. This ritual was always observed. On December 11, however, he was unable to work. On Christmas Day he wrote to (now 'Sir') Edmund Gosse, 'I am in bed on my back, living on butter-broth & beef tea, the servants being much concerned at my not being able to eat any Christmas pudding...'. The local doctor, Sir Henry Head, who was a friend of Hardy, was called, but could discover no specific reason for Hardy's weakness. J.M. Barrie (Scottish playwright and novelist), a friend of longstanding, also arrived from London with offers of help. [16.9]

This was a severe winter, and snow lay deep on the ground. As the evening of January 11 fell, Hardy asked Florence to read to him a verse from the *Rubaiyat* of Omar Khayyam, 'Oh, Thou, who Man of baser Earth didst make... Man's forgiveness give – and take!' In this, Hardy demonstrated that his relationship with the 'Creator' must of necessity be active rather than passive, in other words a two-way process; his Creator must forgive Hardy (his sins), in which case Hardy would do likewise! Hardy died shortly after 9p.m.

17

Aftermath: *Winter Words*

Hardy's ashes were interred in Westminster Abbey, in Poets' Corner at 2p.m. on Monday, January 16, 1928, a spadeful of his beloved Dorset soil being sprinkled on the casket. The last novelist to be buried here prior to this was Charles Dickens in 1870. Hardy had never been introduced to Dickens, a fellow champion of the poor and underprivileged, although he had attended some of his readings at the Hanover Square Rooms in London in the 1860s.

Present at the funeral were Conservative Prime Minister Stanley Baldwin, Leader of the Opposition Ramsay MacDonald, the heads of Magdalene College, Cambridge, and Queen's College, Oxford, and many eminent literary figures of the day, including Sir James Barrie, John Galsworthy, Sir Edmund Gosse, A.E. Housman, Rudyard Kipling and George Bernard Shaw who acted as pall bearers. Also members of the Macmillan publishing house attended, who had organised the event. Florence and Katharine were in attendance, but not so Henry, who was in poor health.

In fact, Henry was at Stinsford Church where, at the same time as the Westminster service, Hardy's heart (which had been previously removed from his body) was being buried in the tomb of Emma, his first wife. On the one side of his tomb was that of his sister Mary, and on the other that of his parents Thomas II and Jemima. Beyond that were buried his grandfather Thomas I, then his grandmother Mary, then his uncle James, and finally his aunt Jane and cousin Theresa. Also simultaneously, a memorial service to Hardy was held in Dorchester, in the presence of the Mayor and Corporation, and many distinguished dignitaries. According to his cousin Teresa, Hardy in life had expressed the wish to be buried at Stinsford 'to lie with his own folk in the churchyard'. However, it was not to be. [17.1]

Florence lived on at Max Gate until her death in 1937. She had two books published: *The Early Life of Thomas Hardy* (1928), and *The Later Years of Thomas Hardy* (1930), both by Macmillan. She is buried in Stinsford churchyard, in the tomb of Hardy and his first wife Emma. Brother Henry also died in 1928, but sister Katharine lived on until 1940.

Hardy's boyhood home, at Higher Bockhampton, now belongs to the National Trust, as does his own former home, Max Gate.

∞

Published by Macmillan in October 1928, nine months after Hardy's death, the collection of poems entitled in *Winter Words* contain yet more poorly disguised sentiments about Emma. 'To Louisa in the Lane', Hardy asks her (presumably Emma) to 'Wait... till with flung off flesh I follow you.'; in, 'Song to Aurore', he affirms that 'love... only leads to pain...'; and in 'The Destined Pair', he ponders on whether Fate would have been, 'kinder... Had he failed to find [meet] her [Emma]...' in the first place.

Epilogue

The genius of Thomas Hardy is multi-faceted; each facet reflecting his brilliance as a diamond reflects the light. His literary and classical allusions are drawn from his immense mental 'data-base' of knowledge, laid down in his mind after years of sustained and devoted study. And yet, he never loses his impish sense of fun. Stories collected by him on his journey through life, from personal observation, newspaper articles, and conversations with others, whether amusing or macabre, were stored away to be woven (sometimes years later) into the tapestry of his novels; and retold with all the rustic wit and wisdom of the true countryman.

The various plots and settings of Hardy's novels were based on original and authentic sources (though he frequently transposed the locations of buildings and characters to suit his own purposes, much to the frustration of his would-be biographers and followers!). Succeeding generations should be eternally grateful to him for leaving an historical record of a way of life which has now largely disappeared. As the lives of his heroes and heroines are played out before us, so beneath the surface lurk the great questions and conundrums with which he himself wrestled during his lifetime: religion, the class system, the law, man's place in the universe, the paradoxical contrast between the fickleness and the faithfulness of human nature, and the mystery of love itself. And nearer to home, those outside influences – usually unwelcome – which were being brought inexorably to bear on his sacred landscape of 'Wessex'.

Hardy's 'characters' are as fresh and colourful today as they were when he sketched them; using a new pencil whenever he commenced a new novel. To us, as to him, they are living creatures, friends even, and we, like him, can identify with their struggle. His legacy, magnificent in itself, is made all the richer as we begin to comprehend the nature of the man, experience with him his emotions, appreciate the enduring beauty and validity of his works, and discover why they are loved and treasured more than ever, the world over.

He has been accused by some of having no sense of humour; seeing only the dark side of life, being depressive, and even morbid, and yet this is to see only one side of him. Sir Newman Flower explains that Hardy 'was drawn towards Tragedy, not by any macabre interest, but by his confusion as to why these things should be'. The 'implacability and mercilessness' of 'Life in punishment' (i.e. in the way it appears to punish certain unfortunate individuals for no apparent reason), were matters which affected Hardy deeply and caused him to be 'stricken inwardly...'. [E1]

Most images of Hardy show him looking serious; but there is one photograph where the mask has slipped, and he has a definite twinkle in his eye – for yes, Hardy could make us laugh, as well as cry – as when the 'Mellstock Quire' went to sleep during a church sermon, then awoke and, believing themselves still to be at a local dance of the night before, sprang into life and played not a hymn, but a jig! Episodes like this show the lighter, vibrant side of Hardy's character.

༄

Hardy's marriage to Emma was the great catastrophe of his life. Never was her insufferable, self-centred, attention-seeking behaviour demonstrated more clearly than during a visit of Henry Newbolt and W.B. Yeats to Max Gate. As representatives of the Royal Society of Literature, they were there to make Hardy a presentation on the Society's behalf. However, so incessantly did Emma regale Yeats with tales of her two cats (which sat on the table beside her plate), as Hardy tried to discuss architecture with Newbolt, that Hardy was obliged to insist that she left the room before the presentation was made! [E2]

Despite Emma's cold and antisocial behaviour, and her attempts to isolate Hardy from his family, he was still able to enjoy concerts and the theatre; bicycling and architecture, and the company of his literary friends; to take an interest in the burning topics of the day, women's suffrage, politics, war; and to write romantically about such colourful characters as Gabriel Oak and Bathsheba!

In his poem, 'He Never Expected Much' (which was a reflection on his eighty-sixth birthday), Hardy admitted that ever since childhood he never expected 'That life would all be fair.' But surely he could not have expected to have to endure the 'contempt' which Emma showed for him, rather than love (verse 2), nor the 'strain and ache' which each new year brought as a result of his association with her (verse 3). This harsh and untoward experience even prompted him to ask whether young women should be informed of the facts of life PRIOR TO marriage, instead of being left to discover them afterwards (and by this he did not mean only the physical side, but also the social and emotional sides). Was marriage 'such a desirable goal for all women as it is assumed to be?', or was it the truth that that particular institution had 'never succeeded in creating that homely thing: a satisfactory scheme for the conjunction of the sexes.' [E3]

In the face of Emma's increasing mental dysfunction Hardy displayed loyalty, tolerance, steadfastness and stoicism. And yet, supposing he had married a happy, loving, caring, well adjusted and outward looking person, would a contented Hardy have been capable of producing works so profound as *Tess of the D'Urbervilles*, *Jude the Obscure*, and *The Dynasts*? If it is in the nature of creative genius that it has of necessity to be born out of pain, then perhaps posterity has something to thank Emma for after all!

∽

What would Hardy have made of modern life? Even in his day he bewailed the coming of industrialisation, in the form of steam traction engines and harvesters, which forced the agricultural labourers off the land. The abolition of his father's beloved 'Quire' of minstrels, the removal of the balcony in Puddletown Church from which they sang, and their replacement with a mechanical organ, caused him immense anguish.

The cry today, as Hardy's precious Dorset fields are steadily and remorselessly swallowed up by estates of new houses and new highways is, for even more roads, houses, hospitals and schools; yet on the other hand, a recent 'liberty and livelihood' pro-countryside march attracted a record 470,000 demonstrators onto the streets of London to protest about the degradation of the aforesaid countryside and its customs. At the root of the problem is the ever increasing density of population (15 million in 1841 – the first year of Hardy's life – in England and Wales, as compared to 52 million in the year 2001), and no doubt Hardy would have been familiar with what the eighteenth-century English population theorist Robert Malthus had to say on the subject! So is there nothing to mitigate the gloom?

After generations of laissez-faire, the education authorities have added 'citizenship' to the 'personal and social education' part of the curriculum. The aim is to dispel ignorance and to encourage pupils from an early age to take responsibility, both for each other and for the environment.

This is a positive sign. In Hardy's time, caring for the environment – the fields, the hedgerows and the animals – was a way of life. The gulf between rich and poor was perhaps no greater in relative terms than it is today, but it was highlighted by the relative paucity of provision for welfare and health. Yet although he loved the pets which he kept at Max Gate, it was with human beings that Hardy was primarily concerned. He enjoyed their music and their laughter, but felt for them in their suffering also, in a deep and genuine way. For him personally, revolution and bloodshed were not the way forward, but rather a quiet application to his writings, which brings to the world a never fading message of love and humanity.

Appendix

5.5	SOMEREC,p.50.	6.10	PBE,ch.37.
5.6	SOMEREC,p.53.	6.11	PBE,ch.20.
5.7	SOMEREC,p.55.	6.12	PBE,ch.37.
5.8	SOMEREC,p.56.	6.13	PBE,ch.2.
5.9	DR,ch.8.	6.14	PBE,ch.36.
5.10	DR,Introduction and	6.15	MEMORIES,p.111.
	ch.1.	6.16	FLOWER,p.94.
5.11	GIT,ch.21.	6.17	PBE,ch.35.
5.12	DR,ch.21.	6.18	PBE,ch.30.
5.13	FEH,p.16.	6.19	PBE,ch.32.
5.14	SOMEREC,p.56.	6.20	PBE,ch.31.
5.15	SOMEREC,p.49.	6.21	PBE,ch.32.
5.16	SOMEREC,p.56.	6.22	PBE,ch.30.
5.17	SOMEREC,p.58.	6.23	PBE,ch.30.
5.18	FEH,p.84.	6.24	PBE,ch.27.
5.19	UGT,ch.2.	6.25	PBE,ch.38.
5.20	UGT,ch.4.	6.26	PBE,ch.7.
5.21	Florence Dugdale to	6.27	PBE,ch.8.
	Edward Clodd, July 3,	6.28	PBE,ch.9.
	1913, Brotherton Library	6.29	PBE,ch.9.
	Collection, University of	6.30	FEH,p.93.
	Leeds.	6.31	FEH,p.96.
		6.32	FMC,ch.4.

CHAPTER 6:

		6.33	FMC,ch.4.
6.1	*The Sunday Times*, Rachel	6.34	FMC,ch.18.
	Dobson, 'Hardy, the copy-	6.35	FMC,ch.6.
	cat of Casterbridge', August	6.36	FMC,ch.10.
	3, 2003. (Thomas Hardy's	6.37	FMC,ch.12.
	Notebook to be published	6.38	FMC,ch.19.
	by Ashgate in 2004).	6.39	FMC,ch.20.
6.2	CL,2,pp.131-3.	6.40	FMC,ch.32.
6.3	PBE,ch.5.	6.41	FMC,ch.37.
6.4	PBE,ch.5.	6.42	FMC,ch.42.
6.5	PBE,ch.22.	6.43	FMC,ch.57.
6.6	PBE,ch.30.		
6.7	PBE,ch.7.		**CHAPTER 7**
6.8	PBE,ch.21.	7.1	CL1,p.31.
6.9	PBE,ch.14.	7.2	EDH,p.12.

7.3	EDH,p.32.	9.3	FEH,p.171.
7.4	CL1,p.33.	9.4	MC,Preface.
7.5	ELH,Diary, 1874-6 (DCM).	9.5	FEH,p.196.
7.6	CL1,p.37.	9.6	MC,Preface.
7.7	THOE,Preface.	9.7	FMC,ch.26.
7.8	FEH,p.106.	9.8	FEH,p.197.
7.9	EHD,1,p.66.	9.9	FEH,p.206.
7.10	THOE,Preface.	9.10	FEH,p.174.
7.11	WEBER,p.68.	9.11	FEH,p.176.
7.12	EH,Diary,2,p.100.	9.12	CL1,p.154.
7.13	RN,ch.9.	9.13	CL1,p.158.
7.14	RN,1:7.	9.14	FEH,p.185.
7.15	RN,3:3.	9.15	WOOD,ch10.
7.16	RN,3:4.		
7.17	RN,4:6.		
7.18	RN,2:3.	**CHAPTER 10**	
7.19	RN,6:4.	10.1	FEH,p.209.
		10.2	CL1,p.190.
		10.3	FEH,p.224.
CHAPTER 8		10.4	CL1,p,205.
8.1	FEH,p.127.	10.5	STEW,p.150.
8.2	TM,ch.16 .	10.6	CL1,p.239.
8.3	TM,Preface.	10.7	FEH,p.237.
8.4	EH,p.176.	10.8	FEH,p.240.
8.5	MILL,p.215.	10.9	TOD,ch.1.
8.6	THNBK,I, p.61.	10.10	TOD,ch.5.
8.7	Bible, Book of	10.11	TOD,ch.41.
	Revelations,iii,14-16.	10.12	TOD,ch.47.
8.8	EH,p.178.	10.13	FEH,p.246.
8.9	FEH,p.153.		
8.10	FEH,p.154.		
8.11	FEH,p.157.	**CHAPTER 11**	
8.12	FEH,p.312.	11.1	CL,1,54.
8.13	*Longmans Magazine*,Vol.2	11.2	CL,2,87.
	1883,pp.252-267.	11.3	JO,Preface.
		11.4	JO,ch.1,pt.1.
		11.5	JO,ch.1,pt.2.
CHAPTER 9		11.6	CL,2,94.
9.1	FEH,p.169.	11.7	CL,2,97.
9.2	FEH,p.170.	11.8	JO,ch.3,pt.6.

11.9 JO,ch.3,pt.4.
11.10 JO,ch.1,pt.3.
11.11 JO,ch.5,pt.1.
11.12 JO,ch.5,pt.4.
11.13 JO,ch.4,pt.3.
11.14 FEH,p.272.
11.15 CL,2,p.104.
11.16 CL,2,p.109.
11.17 CL,2,p.125.
11.18 CL,2,p.124.

CHAPTER 12

12.1 WB,pt.1,ch.2.
12.2 WB,pt.1,ch.9.
12.3 EH,p.254.
12.4 CL,2,p.143.
12.5 CL,2,p.176,178.
12.6 CL,2,p.181.
12.7 CL,2,p.188.
12.8 CL,2,p.187.
12.9 CL,2,p.189.
12.10 CL,2,p.193.
12.11 CL,2,p.194.
12.12 CL,2,p.202.
12.13 CL,2,p.206.
12.14 CL,2,p.208.

CHAPTER 13

13.1 CL,2,p.221.
13.2 CL,2,pp.225,232,238.
13.3 CL,2,p.248.
13.4 CL,2,p.264.
13.5 CL,2.p.269.
13.6 CL,2,pp.282,283.
13.7 FEH p.309.
13.8 CL,2,p.303.
13.9 FLOWER, p.95.
13.10 FEH,p.311.
13.11 CL,3,p.5.

13.12 CL,3,pp.17,19.
13.13 CL,3,p.23.
13.14 CL,3,p.33.
13.15 CL,3,p.46.
13.16 CL,3,p.50.
13.17 CL,3,p.53.
13.18 CL,3,p.58.
13.19 CL,3,p.68.
13.20 CL,3,p.74.
13.21 CL,3,p.110.
13.22 CL,3,p.119.
13.23 CL,3,pp.114-115.
13.24 CL,3,p.130.
13.25 FEH,p.327.
13.26 CL,3,p.213.
13.27 CL,3,p.238.
13.28 FEH pp.333-334.
13.29 CL,3,p.249.
13.30 CL,3,p.253.
13.31 CL,3,p.261.
13.32 DYN,Preface.
13.33 DYN,act7,sceneVIII.
13.34 DYN,volIII,after-scene.
13,35 DYN,act1,sceneV.
13.36 CL,3,p.327.
13.37 CL,3,pp.333,335.
13.38 CL,3,p.343.
13.39 CL,4,p.5.
13.40 CL,4,p.19.
13.41 CL,4,p.21.
13.42 CL,4,p.61.

CHAPTER 14

14.1 'Keynotes', by George
Egerton, annotated by
Thomas Hardy and
Florence Henniker
(collection of Richard

Little Purdy), p.29,30.

14.2 CL,5,p.19.

14.3 TH to Miss Leonie Gifford, Nov.23 1914 (Bristol University Library).

14.4 E. Clodd, diary, Oct. 1 1895 (Alan Clodd).

14.5 D. MacCarthy: Professor Harold Hoffman (Miami University of Ohio) interview.

14.6 M. Robinson to I. Cooper Willis, Dec. 17 1937, DCM.

14.7 MONOG.No.18.

14.8 Professor C.H. Gifford, interview, 1975.

14.9 MONOG.No.14.

14.10 MONOG.No.16.

14.11 MONOG.No.16.

14.12 FEH to Sydney Carlyle Cockerell, Dec. 25 1925.

14.13 ELH to L. Gifford, Oct. 18 1911 (Bristol University Library)

14.14 MILL,p.479.

14.15 MONOG.No.29.

14.16 FLOWER,p.95.

14.17 A.C. Benson, diary, Sept. 5 1912.

14.18 ORFW,p.155.

14.19 TH to Edward Clodd, 14 April 1913 (Berg Collection, New York Public Library). E. Clodd, diary, 25 and 27 April 1913 (Alan Clodd)

14.20 Edward Clodd, diary, July 13 1913 (Alan Clodd).

14.21 REC,p.1,2.

14.22 REC,p.6.

14.23 MILL-LEFH,p.6.

14.24 MILL-LEFH,p.8.

14.25 GIFF,p.115.

14.26 MILL-LEFH,p.10.

14.27 MILL-LEFH,p.15.

14.28 MILL-LEFH,p.26.

14.29 MILL-LEFH,p.48.

14.30 REC,p.12,37.

14.31 COMER.

14.32 www.angelfire.com 19.07.03.

14.33 Comer, R.J.

14.34 www.bullyonline.org 19.07.03.

14.35 www.geocities.com 18.07.03.

14.36 www.geocities.com 18.07.03.

14.37 www.bullyonline.org 19.07.03.

14.38 www.2.health-centre.com 19.07.03.

14.39 www.nimh.nih.gov/ publicat/manic.cfm 08.07.03.

14.40 www.nimh.nih.gov/ publicat/manic.cfm 08.07.03.

14.41 Claybury Asylum records, admission order dated July 26 1919.

14.42 Gifford family information, and R. Gittings, p.188.

14.43 CL,4,p.90.

14.44 CL,4,p.105.

14.45 CL,4,p.107.

14.46	CL,4,p.113.
14.47	CL,4,p.132.
14.48	WEBER,p.165.
14.49	FLOWER,p.96.
14.50	FLOWER,p.96.
14.51	THNBK,2,p.117.

CHAPTER 15

15.1	CL,5,p.16.
15.2	MONOG.NO.5.
15.3	CL,5,p.27.
15.4	MONOG.No.7.
15.5	CL,5,p.30.
15.6	FEH,p.366.
15.7	CL,5,pp.42,46.
15.8	CL,5,p.71.
15.9	CL,5,p.91.
15.10	CL,5,p.135.
15.11	CL,5,p.203.
15.12	FEH,pp.375-6.
15.13	CL,5,p.212.
15.14	FEH,p.378.
15.15	FEH,p.383.
15.16	FEH,p.387.
15.17	CL,5,p.303.
15.18	FEH,p.390.
15.19	CL,p.309.
15.20	CL,6,p.16.
15.21	FEH,p.405.
15.22	FEH,p.407.
15.23	CL,6,p.48.
15.24	FEH,p.415.
15.25	MONOG. Nos.5.6.7.14.

CHAPTER 16

16.1	CL,6,p.169.
16.2	CL,6,p.206.
16.3	CL,6,p.247.
16.4	FEH,p.430.
16.5	FEH,p.431.
16.6	CL,7,p.9.
16.7	CL,7,p.32.
16.8	FEH,p.443.
16.9	CL,7,p.89.

CHAPTER 17

17.1	MONOG.No.12.

EPILOGUE

E1	FLOWER,p.91.
E2	*The Later Life and Letters of Sir Henry Newbolt*, ed. M. Newbolt (London, 1942),pp.666-8.
E3	New Review, June 1894,p.681.

Key to abbreviations:

CL	*The Collected Letters of Thomas Hardy* (in 7 volumes).
COMER	Comer, R.J., *Fundamentals of Abnormal Pshchology*, 1999.
DCM	Dorset County Museum.
EH	Evelyn Hardy, *Thomas Hardy, A Critical Biography*.
EHD	*Emma Hardy's Diaries*, Vols. 1 and 2.
ELH	Emma Lavinia Hardy.
FEH	Florence Emily Hardy, *The Life of*

Thomas Hardy.

FLOWER Flower, Sir Newman, *Just as it Happened.*

GIFF Gifford, Henry, *Thomas Hardy and Emma.*

HAW Hawkins, Desmond, *Hardy, Novelist and Poet.*

HANDS Hands, Timothy, *Thomas Hardy and Stinsford Church.*

MEMORIES MacCarthy, Desmond, *Memories.*

MILL Millgate, Michael, *Thomas Hardy: A Biography.*

MILL-LEFH Millgate, Michael, *Letters of Emma and Florence Hardy.*

MONOG Monographs 1-35, J. Stevens Cox.

ORFW *One Rare, Fair Woman* – Thomas Hardy letters to Florence Henniker.

REC Emma Hardy, *Some Recollections.*

SOMEREC *Some Recollections* by Emma Hardy.

STEW Stewart, J.I.M., *Thomas Hardy: A Critical Biography.*

TH Thomas Hardy.

WEBER Weber, Carl J., *Hardy and the Lady from Madison Square.*

THNBK Thomas Hardy's Notebook.

DR *Desperate Remedies.*

DYN *The Dynasts.*

FMC *Far from the Madding Crowd.*

JO *Jude the Obscure.*

MC *The Mayor of Casterbridge.*

PBE *A Pair of Blue Eyes.*

RN *The Return of the Native.*

THOE *The Hand of Ethelberta.*

TM *The Trumpet Major.*

TOD *Tess of the D'Urbervilles.*

UGT *Under the Greenwood Tree*

WOOD *The Woodlanders.*

(And see also Bibliography)

Bibliography

Benson, A.C., Diary, 5 September 1912 (Magdalene College, Cambridge)

Comer, Ronald J., *Fundamentals of Abnormal Psychology*, Second Edition (Worth Publishers, Inc. 1999).

Dictionary of National Biography, (Oxford University Press, London, 1882).

Egerton, George, *Keynotes* (Garland Publishing Inc., New York & London. Reprint of the 1893 edition published by Roberts Bros, Boston, U.S.A.).

Flower, Sir Newman, *Just as it Happened* (Cassell & Company Ltd, London, 1950).

Gifford, Henry, 'Thomas Hardy and Emma', *Essays & Studies of the English Association*, 1966.

Gittings, Robert, *Young Thomas Hardy* (Penguin Books Ltd, 1975).

Hands, Timothy, *Thomas Hardy and Stinsford Church* (Stinsford Parochial Church Council, 1992).

Hardy, Emma, *Diaries*, edited by Richard H. Taylor (Mid Northumberland Arts Group and Carcanet New Press, 1985).

Hardy, Emma, *Some Recollections* (Oxford University Press, London, 1961). (Quotations by kind permission of the publishers)

Hardy, Evelyn (no relation of Thomas Hardy), *Thomas Hardy: A Critical Biography* (The Hogarth Press, London, 1954).

Hardy, Florence Emily, *The Life of Thomas Hardy* (Macmillan Publishers Ltd, London, 1965).

Hardy, Thomas, *The Collected Letters of Thomas Hardy*, edited by Richard Little Purdy and Michael Millgate, Volumes 1-7 (Clarendon Press, Oxford,1978). (Quotations by kind permission of Professor Michael Millgate)

Hardy, Thomas, *One Rare Fair Woman: Thomas Hardy's Letters to Florence Henniker, 1893-1922*, edited by Evelyn Hardy and F.B. Pinion (Macmillan, 1972).

Hardy, Thomas, *The Complete Poems*, edited by James Gibson (Macmillan Publishers Ltd, London, 1976).

Hardy, Thomas, 'The New Wessex Edition' of his novels, including

Desperate Remedies, Far from the Madding Crowd, The Hand of Ethelberta, Jude the Obscure, A Laodicean, The Mayor of Casterbridge, A Pair of Blue Eyes, The Return of the Native, Tess of the D'Urbervilles, The Trumpet Major, Two on a Tower, Under the Greenwood Tree, The Well-Beloved and *The Woodlanders* (Macmillan London Limited, 1990).

Hardy, Thomas, *Notebook*, edited with notes by Evelyn Hardy (The Hogarth Press, London, 1955).

Hawkins, Desmond, *Hardy, Novelist and Poet* (David & Charles, London, 1976). (Quotations by kind permission of the publishers)

Kay-Robinson, Denys, *The First Mrs Thomas Hardy* (Macmillan London Ltd, 1979).

Lewer, David, *Hardy in Swanage* (Dorset Publishing Company, Wincanton, 1990).

Lewis, Heulyn, and Ginny Lewis, *In the Footsteps of Thomas and Emma Hardy* (The North Cornwall Coast and Countryside Service, 2003).

MacCarthy, Desmond, *Memories* (MacGibbon & Kee, London, 1953).

Millgate, Michael, *Thomas Hardy: A Biography* (Oxford University Press, 1982). (Quotations by kind permission of the publishers)

Millgate, Michael, *Letters of Emma and Florence Hardy* (Clarendon Press, Oxford, 1996).

Pitfield, F.P., *Hardy's Wessex Locations* (Halsgrove, Tiverton, Devon, 1992).

Stevens Cox, J., *Thomas Hardy: Materials for a Study of his Life, Times and Works* Monographs 1-35 (The Toucan Press, Guernsey, 1968).

Stewart, J.I.M., *Thomas Hardy: A Critical Biography* (Longman Group Ltd, London, 1971).

The Story of the Tolpuddle Martyrs (Trades Union Congress, London, 1991).

Weber, Carl J., *Hardy and the Lady from Madison Square* (Colby College Press, Maine, U.S.A., 1952). (Quotations by kind permission of the publishers)

Anna Winchcombe, *Hardy's Cottage* (The National Trust, London, 1981).

Windle, Bertram C.A., F.R.S., F.S.A. *The Wessex of Thomas Hardy* (John Lane, The Bodley Head, London, 1902).